A Young Man's Guide to Life

by

Tom Langdale

Grosvenor House
Publishing Limited

This book is published by
Grosvenor House Publishing Ltd
28-30 High Street, Guildford, Surrey, GU1 3HY.
www.grosvenorhousepublishing.co.uk

A CIP record for this book
is available from the British Library

ISBN 978-1-907211-34-8

Acknowledgements

I would like to thank all the young men who have helped me with my research on this book, and hope it is a testament to their openness on their issues.

Also to my friends and colleagues who have had an invaluable input to the feeling of depth of information I have included in this book.

Finally to my wife who has given me continuous support throughout this project.

Preface

From the age of 14, boys are trying to find the answer to their lives, the world and their place in it. Their parents, family, school, and friends at school are the main sources of information on how to grasp the way ahead, but isn't always made clear.

As young men growing up, they want to take part in all the activities that older boys do – drive cars, ride motor bikes, go out with girls (or boys), play sport, make money, and experience everything that life has to offer. The knowledge they need to do all of those things is out there, but they don't always know how to get it.

The reason for writing this book is to enlighten young men with some of the knowledge of life that I craved when I was young. There seemed to be a mountain of information that I needed to know to get me through my early manhood.

There are many books and magazines for girls and women, providing all the knowledge and advice they might need on many subjects. For men, there is very little, and for boys, even less – only sex magazines and problem pages. Although these magazines are part of the typical teenage reading matter, they do not provide all the suitable knowledge that a young man needs to have a more informed development. A couple of useful books have been published recently for boys. I will list them at the back of this book to complement the information you can obtain.

I wanted to ride a motorbike at 13, and also drive a car. I was too young, but time would change that, and I would still need the knowledge to do these things, as I would need the knowledge for everything else I wanted and needed to do.

Girls were starting to feature prominently in my thoughts, but I knew very little about them and this is possibly the most confusing of all areas for an adolescent to understand.

Information on sex, girls, and life issues are crucial to the young man growing up. Therefore, I have researched the modern young man to find out what subjects are problematic and which issues are stressful and cause anxiety.

I have tried to give more of the information needed to help young men gain the ability to maximise their potential and to enjoy their youth to the full.

I have also tried to answer some of the questions that no one wanted to tell me, which I needed to know to stem my own confusion.

My aim in this book is to inform, rather than to advise – so that when you, as a young man, have read this book, you will have some of the tools and building blocks of knowledge to get more out of your young life, in a more confident and less stressful way. This will help you to go out there and experience it all for yourself.

I hope that you will be able to pick up this book at any time, and read the chapters that relate to your need for knowledge on a particular subject. Some of the information in this book you will not need at 14. The buying a house chapter, for example, you may not need till you are older – but you may need the information on bullying at both ages.

However, there is no harm in reading any chapter. You can refer back to it at any time, when the need arises.

Enjoy this book. I hope it gives you pleasure, informs you, and helps clarify some of the issues you may have been concerned about.

Index

CHAPTER 1

Living with your parents

Living with your parents can be a mixed blessing, but as a young teenager, you don't have much choice. You are still in need of that very special nurturing that only your mother and father can give, whether you like it or not.

If you handle your parents right, they can be your friends and benefactors for the rest of their lives.

Mums will always love you and care for you, even when you have a wife, because no girl is ever going to be good enough for her little boy and do all the things that mums do.

She will enjoy entertaining your friends en masse, just to prove to them how lucky you are, having a mum like her. Any friend of yours is a friend of your mum's. However, she will probably tell you if there is a friend she does not approve of.

It is up to you how you respond to your parents' opinions of your friends, but it is a good idea to take on board what they say, and not be confrontational. It can backfire on you. Parents can withdraw favours that you need.

Do make sound judgements and choose your friends carefully. Some boys can be trouble, and you may not see their faults straight away. Any trouble they may get into, you could be led into, and this could reflect on you for the rest of your life. You can get cautions from the police for what you may consider fun. Some of these fun activities are now criminal offences. For example, streaking, flashing and mooning can get you onto the sex offenders' register, so be careful what you do.

Getting a criminal record is one kind of trouble you can do without, and if that ever happens, it will impact on you and your future – there will be certain jobs you will not be allowed to do. Employers will want to know if you have a criminal record. This means that, whenever you apply for a job, it will come up on your application form.

If you ever have the misfortune to go to prison, you will find out what unpleasant places they are: highly stressful and far from the family you love. The subsequent impact on you getting the good job you need to afford the lifestyle you want is obvious, so make wise choices when it comes to friends and the things you do with them.

Not every boy has the advantage of a good family life and the support he needs to keep out of trouble. If you are one of those boys, talk to your mates, teachers or doctors and see what help is there for you. There are help lines for your support. It may be hard but do talk and be proactive for yourself. (Help lines are listed at the back or this book)

Your father can be your mate and you can enjoy the closeness of a friendship that will transcend to your friends in the activities you do together.

Nights out with the boys, playing sport of whatever kind, golf, fishing, shooting, skiing and horse riding are just a few activities that you and your dad can enjoy together. The relationship you have with your father is up to you and how you respond to his nature and his nurture of you is a very personal decision.

Your dad can generally afford a car, and this, to a young man, can be crucial in those early days, when you need transport. Dads will lend their cars, but there will more than likely be "conditions" attached (no alcohol, cleaning it, if you bend it, you pay for it). They may not lend you the Jaguar, but they may lend you the smaller family car. Be grateful – beggars can't be choosy.

If you do borrow mum's or dad's car, drive it carefully. Graveyards are full of kids who thought that they were Michael Schumacher.

Consider all things you do as a young man with care. Have fun, but don't be rash, because survival is the name of the game.

When you're living with your parents, you must realize how much they save you on living costs. They may charge you a small rent or housekeeping money if you are at work, but it will be nothing like the real cost of living on your own. I will cover living alone later on in this book, in Chapter 3.

Ask as many questions of your parents as you can. Their knowledge is also great, and they know you and how you may respond to certain ideas.

Treat your parents with respect. Whatever you've done and whatever you've found out, they have done it before you. They have been there and got the T-shirt.

While you're still at home, get your parents to teach you how to cook and how to iron your own shirts. Your mother may be surprised that you want to learn this kind of stuff, but when you are living on your own, cooking and caring for yourself, you will need these skills. You will make mistakes and burn the proverbial King Arthur's cakes, and ruin the odd item of clothing when ironing, but a bit of practice, under your mum's guidance, won't hurt. I will cover cooking for yourself later in this book, in Chapter 4).

Your parents are a reservoir of knowledge

Learn all you can from your parents. Being able to cook a romantic meal for your girlfriend, or help her with some DIY item she is having trouble with, is a serious plus for a girl when assessing a would be boyfriend's good points. This may seem irrelevant to you now, but when you are on your own and fending for yourself, all these factors will be important.

There are downsides to living at home with your mum and dad. Mums tend to nag you about keeping yourself clean and keeping your room tidy. Don't fight it – this is important to you. When you start going out with girls, dirty hands and dirty underpants are a definite turn off.

When you are a young teenager, taking girls home is not generally a problem, but as you get older, your parents can cramp your style. Not all parents are normally enlightened to the fact that you may want to take your girlfriend up to your room for the purpose of sex. Their embarrassment and insecurity about the situation could prevent this.

If you have a sister, it could be even more difficult, because they wouldn't like their daughter – your sister – to be in the same situation as your girlfriend.

Unfortunately, there is still a double standard when it comes to the freedom of sexual attitudes regarding girls, especially by parents of girls. Dads are very protective of their daughters where boys are concerned, so it may be wise to get dads to like and trust you.

My suggestion is to just be yourself, mums and dads can spot a fraud a mile off. A natural charm is a good characteristic to develop and will certainly help you with the mums. Being polite may seem old fashioned and out of date, but good manners are essential if you want to impress the parents. Open doors for the ladies when getting into a car and when out at pubs and restaurants. It's a natural thing to do, and the modern girl does still like the attention.

It also helps when you are at work if you know how to treat people well and are polite. It goes a long way to saying something about you and how you care for others. Politeness helps to breed charm and confidence.

You can test your charm on your own mother, at home or when you go out. You could even ask her what she thinks of how charming you are - mums like a charming son. She will tell you what girls want as far as charm, is concerned. It will help if you like your mum and like people in general, as charm is developed by being considerate and caring about people.

Bogus charm is also easily spotted, so be aware. It is too easy to sound like a second-hand car salesman with all the right chat. Be sincere, because if you feel what you say, it will sound true and be believed.

When living at home, take the opportunity to save money. At some point, you will want your independence and to be your own man. Also, you may outstay your welcome and your parents may want their own space for the first time since you were born.

Saving can be a challenge when you're young. You want to go out and enjoy yourself, and putting money away seems an impossible thing to do.

Do try and save while you're living at home, because if you go and live on your own in rented housing, you will have little chance to do so, as rents are so high. I will cover buying and renting a house or flat later in this book, in Chapter 3).

Bank Account and money control

Opening up a bank or building society account, under the guidance of your parents, could be a good way of starting, and getting into the saving mind set. One thing that banks like is a developed history of saving over time. This shows your ability to handle your own money. When you apply for a loan, this will be important to a bank or lender. (As a matter of information, Bank savings interest is usually lower than at a building society, so search for the best interest saving rates).

Never trust banks. Their first motive for acquiring your business is profit, and they will charge you for everything if you are not very careful.

Question every charge and make sure you understand any account contract you sign up to. If you don't understand, ask lots of questions. Remember that you are the customer and that bankers are not God. If you're unsure of anything, ask your parents for advice.

One area to be aware of is credit cards. They can get you into a lot of trouble and debt. If you are a good customer, the banks will increase the amount of credit you can have on your card. Resist the spending urge.

Credit cards are the most expensive way of borrowing money.

We always intend to pay the card bill on time, but life has a habit of running away with time and before you know it, you have a whacking great bill and no money to pay it off. The interest card companies charge is very high and it will kick in if you are just one day late in paying your card bill, and you could be paying as much as 25% plus for the privilege.

The safest way is to pay using your current account card only, and to make sure that you have sufficient funds to cover the new purchase in your bank account. (Banks will make a charge for a payment from your account if it has insufficient funds in it to clear that payment).

If you do get into trouble with money, don't ignore it, because the problem won't go away. Talk to your parents. True, they won't be happy, but they will advise you. If that fails, talk to the bank – but don't be intimidated by them. At this point, you have the high ground: it's their money that you have and they will want it back. Negotiate a lower interest rate for the period of repayment. If you don't own anything the bank cannot seize any of your property, they have nothing to take, so they will listen to any offer you make regarding repayment.

If you get into serious money difficulties, bankruptcy is an alternative to clearing your debt. This means declaring that you have no money and no way of paying back your debts – but this method may have some repercussions when you're applying for a loan in the future. You will find it difficult to get a loan, and you won't be clear of your bankrupt status for three to five years. Seek legal advice on any action you take in this field.

If your dad is handy with his hands, learn from him. Everything in your own house, when you buy it, may need attention and will cost you money. Decorating, electrics, and plumbing, just to mention a few, are expensive services to pay for. The more you can do yourself, the more money you can save. Offer to help your dad when he next decorates the lounge. He may be surprised and he may even offer to pay you a little cash, which would be an added bonus.

There is a whole world of knowledge that you can learn at home. You can even learn from your brothers and sisters. They may not readily answer questions, but observe them, see how they respond to certain situations, and make use of their life experience.

If your parents have any kind of a library, use it: read all you can on subjects that are important to you and your survival in the outside world.

Try not to argue with your parents, it is self-defeating and seldom helps, as everyone ends up angry and frustrated. Listen to what they have to say – you may learn something, because knowledge is power and the root of all success.

CHAPTER 2

Living with Friends

The decision to leave home is a big one and should not be taken lightly. Your independence will cost you money.

You will probably have to share a flat or house because of the cost, so your choice of roommate, flat sharer or house sharer is an important one. You have to live with these people day to day and the reality can be very different to what friends are like down the pub or in a social environment.

History has told us that two or more people sharing a house or flat can present many difficulties. What starts as a friendship can soon deteriorate into serious disagreement over the running of the accommodation. If you do not get on 100 per cent with your prospective roommate before you start sharing a house, it is unlikely to improve in what must be a sharing and unselfish environment.

Make sure you know them well and that you can trust them and that you lay down some ground rules. You can point out that it is in their own interest to do so, because you, too, will also be bound by the same rules.

Bill sharing is one of the most contentious issues. Make sure you read the gas and electric meters on taking over a place to live and when you leave. Also, date your readings. These bills should be shared equally: we all do similar things around the house, such as cooking, showering, and turning on heating, and over the year, these bills will even out.

Telephone bills are a little different. We all use phones, but some more than others – so stick to using your own mobile. A house phone is unnecessary and you will have eliminated the most contentious of all household bills.

Council tax also has to be paid by the tenant and should be shared, but water charges are usually paid by the landlord.

Job sharing in keeping the home tidy is possibly a good idea, but it doesn't always work. Human nature being what it is we tend to leave household chores to someone else and if you think that by sharing with a girl, the problem is solved, think again. Single girls are as messy as single boys and sometimes worse.

Your choice of a place to live is also important. If you move in with a friend or find a place with a friend, make sure that you can afford it and that you are both happy with the location and type of accommodation you have chosen.

If you do choose to rent, remember that landlords take a dim view of late payment of rent and this may impact on your ability to obtain a reference for a future tenancy.

Landlords cannot start eviction proceedings until you are two months behind with your rent, so assure your landlord that your financial situation is a temporary one and that you will pay any arrears.

Try to be truthful and do what you say you are going to do when dealing with people where money is concerned. If you lie and are found out, they won't trust you again.

If you are going to rent a place to live, you will be asked to sign a lease. This is normal. The period of time is generally up to you. Six months to a year is reasonable to start with but do avoid long term. Your circumstances may change and you may be stuck with years to run on a lease for which you are responsible.

You will also be asked to pay a deposit of about one and half times a month's rent for the landlord's security of property and fittings. Landlords historically have suffered large financial losses because of damage to their property by tenants. It is a serious problem for landlords and if you damage anything that belongs to them, it will be deducted from your deposit.

Deposits have to be held by a third party, due to some horror stories of unscrupulous landlords retaining all the deposit unreasonably. It is now law that landlords have to belong to a protected deposit scheme, and the penalties for not doing so are high.

I will cover cooking for yourself later in this book, but one point that is relevant is that food in the kitchen can be seen as available for all, so make sure that the ground rules you decide on include designated storage space in cupboards and in the fridge. Food going missing can be a major source of arguments.

The costs of living on your own are significantly higher than living with your parents, so distance to your work is the first thing to look at in keeping costs down. Transport costs being what they are, the closer to work you live, the less it costs. Also, going out for entertainment is another consideration. If you are central to where it happens for you, this will also cut costs.

Room and flat prices vary a lot, so shop around. Local newspapers and estate agents will have lists of places to let. Get all the information you can get before choosing.

Furniture is a major issue. If you have access to some second-hand bits and pieces that are useful, get them. Furniture is expensive, and not all flats are furnished.

Most flats have carpets and curtains, but these, too, are expensive. Check with your estate agent or landlord about whether these items are included, so you are prepared with all possible costs.

Whatever you do, think about it carefully. Living with friends can be fun and will enhance your personal development and interpersonal skills a great deal, but people and conditions change.

The main causes of failure in cohabiting with others are selfishness and immaturity and the inability to see the other person's point of view. Try to see all situations from the other person's point of view and talk it through – there is no substitute for it.

If your first time away from home is when you go to university, all of the conditions above apply, but you may not know all the people you live with. You will be unsure of yourself during this life change to start with, but be assured that you're not alone. Everyone feels the same at this point. You won't know how things work and where things are, so talk to and support each other, ask questions and have fun learning about how the big wide world works.

One thing you will need at university is self-motivation. It's not like school, where teachers pressure you. The responsibility to get yourself to where you have to be is yours. If you don't go to lectures, it will be you who loses out. This is a massive culture change, so plan your work, as well as your fun.

Money will be in short supply, so buy your food carefully. You may choose to share your food and cooking to save time and money. This is something you can work out with your new house mates. All of these issues can be made easier if you support and understand each other, because you are all probably experiencing living on your own for the first time. Most of all, with all the things you do, have fun! This is a time of your life that you will never forget.

Chapter 3

Living on your own
and buying a home

Going out into the big wide world can be daunting, and living on your own or with a wife or partner is also a big step to take. Apart from the cost, it is a lifestyle choice. If you choose to be on your own, it is a personal thing, so make sure that it is what you want. Too much time on your own is not good for you. We all need interaction with our fellow human beings.

On the other hand, independence - having the run of your own home and space – is priceless. Being able to invite friends in at the time of your choice is the ultimate luxury, and you can be as tidy or as much of slob as you please.

The decision to buy your first property will also seem quite daunting: it will probably be the biggest and most expensive single item you will ever buy.

There are so many properties to choose from and deciding what to buy and how you buy can be difficult.

When looking for a new home and talking to the vendors, (people who are selling) you will have to hone your negotiating skills to a fine degree to cope with some of the prices that people try to get for their houses. You can quite often talk down the asking price by quite a good sum. If the property has been on the market for some time, it can indicate that the price is too high. Your first point of call is the building society or bank, to see how much you can borrow in relation to what you earn, and how much you have saved toward the property of your choice.

The money you borrow for a house purchase is called a mortgage.

Borrowing levels vary from as low as two and a half times your annual salary (this is the norm, and is the safest), to as much as five, or even seven times your salary. Do not borrow more than you can afford to pay back each month. Your monthly mortgage repayment should be equal to one week's salary.

This will enable you to set your price range of property to look for. Your savings, less legal costs, taken away from the price of the home you want, is the amount you have to borrow. Also remember the other costs involved in setting up your home, such as buying furniture.

Interest rates – the amount that the banks and building societies charge for lending you money – can also vary.

There are so many varying rates and deals that you should shop around for the best one that suits you. Try not to cut corners on your research, because there are hundreds of deals out there and you can save yourself a lot of money with the right lender.

No one can choose a property for you, but you can ask your parents and friends for their opinion, as there may be a factor about the property you have overlooked. You can easily be swept away by the feel of a property that you like and not notice any faults it may have.

Location is the most important factor in determining the price of a property, so it's important to fully investigate the local area of a property that interests you. Get your property surveyed by a professional, but do not let him fob you off with a visual inspection. A surveyor can sometimes inspect a property and then suggest that you hire other professionals to look at it as well, such as plumbers and electricians. Make the inspector responsible for what he or she reports on. Otherwise, the survey is not worth the paper it's written on. If you know a surveyor who has building trade experience, ask them to take a look for you.

With HIPS, (Home information pack) the new questionnaire that vendors have to fill in now, it's a lot safer buying a property, because sellers have to state any faults that they are aware of, which makes them legally responsible for the stated condition of the home.

You will need a solicitor or a qualified conveyance person to process the purchase of your property – the latter is generally less expensive.

Solicitors work to stricter guidelines. This makes them more expensive, and it may take them longer to process your property.

Having decided on who will process your house purchase, ask the conveyance company for a cost estimate, so you know what to budget for. It is important to know all costs up front – that way; there will be no nasty surprises. Also, check the council tax cost and average gas and electricity amounts, water rates. These will all help you budget more accurately. Don't forget you will need a TV licence.

Once you've bought your property, you have to knock it into the sort of shape that suits you and your space, and try to get it to reflect the kind of lifestyle you want for yourself.

This will also cost you money, and an ideal space may have to wait, but you will still have to furnish your property to some level, which is expensive. Carpets, curtains, furniture, cooker and a fridge are some of the items you will need. A dishwasher is not essential – you have two hands.

One way of cutting the cost of a mortgage is to rent a room to a friend or colleague. This means that you have to buy a property with more than one bedroom. The ideal property is a three bedroom semi-detached house, but it may be out of your reach, so do your sums, because it may be more cost effective to let two bedrooms. It may be an idea to consider a three bedroom terrace. The prices of these properties are a little lower and do vary. It could make economic sense, but do your homework to see what suits you.

The same principle applies for buying as for letting: choose your tenant carefully.

There will be tax to pay on rental income, so check with Inland Revenue how much it is likely to be. 25% has been normal in the past, but subject to changes by government, less the cost of setting up to let part of your house or flat. There are special tax rules for letting income, so be careful what you claim for on your tax return. If you're unsure, consult an accountant for the correct advice.

The primary factor when you are buying a property is the amount of savings you will need, so you should put a part of your earnings away as soon as possible. You will need a lot of money to do all the things you want to do, so try not to waste any money on things you do not really need.

Two sure ways of wasting money are cigarettes and alcohol. Although you need to have fun, cigarettes are totally unnecessary, apart from being very bad for you. **Alcohol** is different: it is not good for you in large quantities, but in sensible amounts, it can be fun. However, it is expensive. Pubs and clubs charge far too much for drinks, so limit your drinking to the saving goals you have set for yourself. This, in reality, is very, very hard – you are young and you want to live a little. But bear in mind that every drink you buy is profit for someone else, and that money is not in your savings account.

Owning a car is expensive and will take a lot of your money to keep on the road. Learn to drive, but do your sums on the economics of public transport costs against car costs.

Do draw a balance between saving and fun time – you are only young once.

One good way of saving more is to take on another job. You could do a job that is semi-social – for example, working behind a bar, or anywhere that you can meet people; friends and possibly girlfriends. Or turn a hobby into an earner. Whatever it is, all the time you are working, you are not spending.

When you have bought your home, you will need to insure it. This is something the mortgage company will insist on. If you are lucky enough to buy your home outright, it is still advisable to insure it, as you never know what may happen in the future and you do not want to lose your most valuable asset.

There are many insurance companies, so shop around for the most detailed cover relative to the cost you have to pay. This is called your insurance premium. You can also get the contents of your home insured with the building. This is sometimes a cheaper way of doing it.

Get many prices from different companies, making sure that the companies you get quotes from are secure. Ask questions and research online to establish the soundness of the insurance company you choose. Using the larger, well-known companies is probably safest, but this could cost you a little more.

Get your choice of who supplies your gas and electricity. There are many companies eager to supply you, so do your homework and find out who will give you the best deal.

You could buy a flat or house with a friend, as another way of gaining some independence. If this is the best way for you, make sure you choose the right friend and that you both can afford to keep up the payments.

If you don't keep up the mortgage payments, you could lose your property.

If you default on your mortgage, the bank or building society will repossess and sell your property, generally at a loss, so you could be homeless and in debt.

If you are unlucky enough to lose your house, you will need to Store your belongings and find somewhere else to live. It can be a harsh world out there, so seek help from friends and family before this happens. There is generally another way out.

Alternatively, you may be able to buy the other share of the house if your friend can no longer afford to pay, and you could let the other room to help pay the extra mortgage payments.

Although you cannot foresee any down-turn in your earning power, if it does happen, talk to your mortgage lender as soon as possible.

Mortgage companies will generally be sympathetic to a temporary non-payment. They will, if applicable, reschedule your loan – but do make every effort to resolve the financial situation you may be in. Building societies and banks are not charities, and they will take a business-like view of any situation, so proceed carefully.

If you have done all your homework on the property of your choice, and the costs and implications on your ability to establish yourself as an independent person, you should be able to make that step a lot easier and less stressful. With all the knowledge you have gained from your research of your needs and the way ahead, you will be content with the result and ready to enjoy your future home.

CHAPTER 4

Caring for yourself

When we are young, we can worry about our health and how we can keep ourselves on top of feeling good. We sometimes think about dying and when this will happen. None of us know the answer to that question, but it does not help to dwell on something we cannot change. We will all die at some point in time. The trick is to enjoy the time that we have until then.

One good way to ensure that we live a long time is to feed ourselves properly, and exercise to keep fit.

The modern, prepared food that supermarkets sell makes it very simple to feed yourself, which is the primary point in caring for yourself. Your internal engine needs fuel and you cannot function without it.

I am not going to write a cookery book for you because, there are a lot of cookery books out there for singles or couples that you can buy, written by experts.

What I can do is tell you that there is no great secret to doing your own cooking.

The key is planning your meal. Meat, vegetables, pastas and rice are good base ingredients for a quick meal. When I was single, I could usually eat my meal within 20 minutes of starting cooking.

As an example,

4oz Beef steak
1 good size potato
Choice of green vegetables

Peel the potato and cut into four pieces, and put them on to boil in a saucepan with slightly salted cold water. Cook for 20 minutes. While the potatoes are cooking, prepare your vegetables – for instance, cabbage or broccoli – wash under cold water, slice into small strips or florets and add to slightly salted boiling water. Typically, vegetables will take five to seven minutes to cook.

Wash the steak under cold water and dry it with kitchen towel. Fry or grill it with a light cover of salt and black pepper. You could also add a sliced garlic clove for more flavour. If you fry the steak, only use oil and don't have it too hot. Turn down the gas or electric cooker a little and turn the steak regularly through an eight to 10-minute cooking time. Serve with mustard for the steak and butter for the potatoes.

You could have peas with your steak, which is even easier. Take the right amount of peas out of the packet to suit your taste, add to a small amount of salted boiling water and cook for three to five minutes.

Another easy dish is pasta in sauce with salad. If you serve this up for a girlfriend, she will be impressed.

Cook two to three ounces of tagliatelle per person, adding it to a saucepan of slightly salted boiling water. Cook for seven to ten minutes. While the pasta is cooking stir occasionally while you are preparing your salad, so it does not stick to the bottom of the saucepan.

To prepare the salad, wash the lettuce leaves and slice into small strips, wash and slice up a few tomatoes, remove the skin from part of a cucumber and cut into slices, clean and slice a couple of spring onions, put into a salad bowl and mix up together. You can buy salad dressing to suit your own taste, but another option is one you can make for yourself. I was given an old recipe some years ago for French vinaigrette, and my family uses this dressing all the time.

Vinaigrette Recipe: 1 pinch of salt, add pepper to taste
$^1/_4$ teaspoon of powdered mustard
2 tablespoons of malt vinegar
4 tablespoons of vegetable oil

Mix all the ingredients together. Add the vinaigrette to the salad and mix well. When the pasta is cooked, drain off the water and mix in a jar of pasta sauce, while reheating again for a few minutes over a low heat, stirring continuously, then serve. The mix-in sauce can be bought at any supermarket, and the result is quick and delicious.

These are samples of how you can cook for yourself. It's very easy if you follow the instructions on the packets or jars of the ingredients that you buy. The cookery books that are in the shops have detailed instructions, so don't be put off by what may seem like complex meals.

There are many things to take into consideration when cooking and keeping things clean. When preparing meat, use a plastic cutting board, as wooden ones absorb germs and bacteria which are hard to get rid of. Do not store different meats together in the same container. Chicken and pork are the most liable to carry germs in their raw state; always cook them well. If you're in doubt about the freshness of a product, throw it away.

Pre-cooked meals or products should be cooked through until piping hot. If they are not heated through, bacteria can be activated at certain temperatures.

A microwave oven is also a handy piece of kitchen equipment. There are many meals you can cook quickly by microwave and all cooking instructions are on the packet.

When you feel more confident, you can experiment with cooking ideas of your own. If you are unsure, ask the woman in your life. She will be only too pleased to help.

It is essential that you eat a balanced diet to keep healthy, and eating fruit and vegetables is a must. Your general health and looks can be affected without these balanced ingredients.

After you have cooked, there is generally a mess left behind. Clean it up. There is nothing worse than coming down to the kitchen in the morning to a sink full of dirty pots and pans.

This also counts in the bedroom. If all the rooms in the house are clean and tidy, you will be surprised how much better you will feel personally. Cleanliness reflects on your self-esteem. It is paramount that you keep yourself and anything that is yours clean and tidy. The spin-off in confidence is incalculable. Look good, feel good!

Duster, mop, washing machine and vacuum cleaner are the basic tools. Cleaning liquid, polish and washing powder for your clothes are some of the materials you will also need. Luckily, all of these items have instructions on how to use them – because there are so many cleaning products, I would have to write another book just for instructions if I told you how to use every product.

It is very difficult to imagine young men keeping themselves and their home clean. It is not the natural order of things, but do try. Whipping around the house with a duster and vacuum cleaner doesn't take long and there is always free time at some point during the week.

Wipe the surfaces of your furniture with a duster and shake it outside, making sure that the wind outside does not blow the dust back in your face.

Empty the vacuum cleaner bag or dust container regularly. The vacuum cleaner is a simple piece of equipment to use. The one thing to watch out for is knocking into furniture and skirting boards – doing so may chip or damage these surfaces. Make sure you keep hold of the cable and guide it away from the sweeper head. If you run over the cable, you could damage it and you could electrocute yourself or start a fire, so take care.

All this cleaning is the first part of taking care of the inner self. Your emotional well-being is as important as the physical self.

Keeping yourself strong inside is achieved by what you feel about yourself and most of this is given to you by your parents, which you build on.

The way they brought you up and the confidence they gave you are the building blocks of self-worth and emotional stability as an adult.

If you were lucky and received the all-encompassing, personality-building and nurturing by your parents, then you should have no problems in coping with the outside world. If the reverse is true, then keeping those moments of self-doubt in check can be difficult – but rest assured, the most confident of people also have doubts.

Always think positively. There is no such phrase as, "I can't do that". If you can't do something, then find out how. The knowledge to do every known thing is out there somewhere. Say to yourself, "I can do this", but only if it is important to you. Don't climb Everest for someone else – do it for yourself.

You are the most important person to you, and when you look in the mirror, reassure yourself of the fact that there is one person in that mirror that you care about – care about him and then you can care about others.

Internal verbalising is something we all do, but some of it is negative. Going over and over a particular problem in your head can tie you up in knots. We can't always sort out our problems ourselves. If this is the case, talk to friends, parents, or a counsellor – it will ease your inner strife.

Confident people ask questions all the time – that's how they learn. They get answers to issues, and this, in turn, reduces their stress. Knowledge is power – self-power.

There is never a quick fix for our inner strength; we have to work at it. Carrying emotional baggage is one of the most destructive influences we can suffer. If we can learn to compartmentalise these feelings and understand each issue, we can move on with life without tormenting ourselves with historical mental weights.

If a problem can be solved, first break it down into smaller pieces, then, solve the problem, bits at a time. If it can't be solved, forget it. The old saying is true: "It's no good worrying about what you can't change."

One of the biggest mistakes we make is putting off until tomorrow that which we can do today. If something is worrying you, sort it out straight away – that way, your grief time is shortened to a minimum and generally the problem we thought was serious turns out to be simply solved.

If you have a more serious problem, talk about it. If you feel that you can't talk to your parents, then see a professional. There is no merit in suffering in silence and on your own. Never hold back when talking to a doctor or counsellor. Say what you feel – that's what they're paid for.

Another important way of caring for your inner self is the internal and external physical self and the need to keep fit. Healthy body, healthy mind as the saying goes – so try and exercise regularly. The feel-good factor that exercise will give you comes from the endorphins that are produced in your body when you work out. The basic act of exercise gives you a direct physical and mental lift, and the gains are enormous.

If you exercise when you're feeling stressed, this can help disperse adrenaline. This is the chemical that stress produces and if you do regular exercise, it helps to counteract the effects of this chemical. Exercise is also good for maintaining your cardiovascular health.

Sometimes we do things that are not good for our health, such as smoking and drinking. They will affect your health by reducing the efficiency of your internal organs and your cardiovascular system, and this can cause serious illness.

All the things that I have mentioned are there to help you do the best for yourself, and do the best you can to take care of yourself. Think through what you want to do in keeping yourself fit and well. Being fit and healthy will make you more able to handle life and all that it has to throw at you.

CHAPTER 5

Self-Esteem

That feel-good factor is sometimes an elusive quality that everyone except you seems to have.

Fear not – we are all the same: we all have our down moments, and we all worry about feeling good about ourselves. Generally, we are OK, but this feeling doesn't stay all the time, and this is normal. We all need to learn about who we are, before we can limit the insecure feelings and down time.

None of us feel good about ourselves all the time, because things happen to us that change how we feel about ourselves. What we need to do is build up our self-esteem, so that we can handle the low times and keep them in perspective.

The problem that all teenage boys have is that they are turning into men, with all the body changes that entails. Your voice gets deeper, your testicles drop and you start growing hair everywhere, beginning with the pubic and facial areas.

What is more disturbing and hard to handle are the emotional changes, as your feelings from boy to man kick in. You begin to wonder where you fit in the order of things, and how you can understand what is going on, and how you can become that individual you want to be. You feel the need to have thoughts and opinions of your own, apart from your parents; in your own right as an individual.

Gaining your independence from your parents is sometimes the hidden motive for mood changes, and the starting of arguments. Not doing what your parents ask is a way of asserting yourself – finding out who that person is that you want to be.

This is a difficult time. You will have mood swings, and will start being lippy to your mum and dad. You will possibly become a rebel in the way that you behave. You might go out drinking and get drunk, smoke, try drugs, come in late, or not do your school work or homework. All of this is normal in the effort to gain your identity and your sense of self, but this can be a very destructive time when it comes to your future and self-esteem.

To help you understand what you are going through, it may be useful to know that your brain is reprogramming itself to take on board all the changes to your body and thoughts that you are experiencing. You will become self-absorbed – you will only think of yourself and develop selfish traits. You will only see your own point of view on any subject. You will wonder why your parents do not do everything you want them to do, or let you do all that you want to do.

This is a time of steep learning, and it will go on until your brain has reprogrammed itself, and will hopefully be completed from your 20s onward and is usually done by the time you're 25.

The trick is to survive this time, because you will have a lot of experiences and do some good things and some mad things on your journey to adulthood.

Don' worry about this change you are going through,

as we all have to do it, but by knowing what is happening to you, you can think about what you do and adjust your behaviour to keep yourself safe and limit the damage to you and your self-esteem.

Feeling good about yourself is a state of mind and should be taken for granted, but because of what is going on in your head and body, it will be hard. It will take time and have to be worked at.

We all have the right to be alive and to be self-determinate in what we want and do. Through this journey, don't lose sight of who you are and what you stand for. Having strong views and opinions is a way of finding where you fit in the order of things. Listening to others is an important method of finding out what is important to you and the development of your views, and your opinions during this learning time.

Having listened to others and formed a strong sense of self, it is a show of strength to be able to readjust your view if another point of view is pointed out to you, with which you agree and which is better suited to who you want to be. To be able to see the other person's point of view represents a position of wisdom and strength.

Another way of building on your view of yourself and developing your self-esteem is how you look and behave. This has a large influence on how you and others think about you. Looking good makes you attractive, and being attractive to women is fundamental to a boy or man's feeling of self-worth.

We don't all look like Brad Pitt, so our attractiveness to women has to be worked on. Feeling good and confident is attractive to women, even if you don't always feel it. Practice what makes you feel good in the mirror at those getting ready to go out moments. Talk to the mirror; tell yourself how good you are. The Fonz in *Happy Days* and John Travolta in *Saturday Night Fever* did it. It seemed to work for them and why not. (These films are old, so you may not know who these people are, but look them up and watch the films – it will give you some idea of the kind of self-belief we all should have.)

The confidence you gain from doing your hair and putting on your new clothes is all building that feel-good factor that we need for ourselves.

When we have done all that preparation on how we look, it is important not to behave like a prat. One way that people judge you is on what you say. The mouth is a slippery place and words can come out of it before we have put our brain into gear.

If alcohol affects your ability to talk sense, limit your intake. Being drunk is not attractive to women and does not help you build your confidence and the feeling of who you are. Stay sober and be ahead of the game.

We can sometimes feel intimidated by crowds and not want to give our opinion, because we feel shy, or are frightened of making a fool of ourselves. These feelings are common in the young and quite normal. You have not yet gained those interpersonal skills that can only come with practice.

If you listen to what is being said and don't worry about how you feel, you may find yourself joining in naturally. You could practice with smaller groups to see how you get on. This will help to build self-esteem and enable you to join in, unaffected by the number of people around you.

Sometimes we can talk just to one person, and that can make us nervous. Especially if that person is a she, and someone that we really like, that feeling of nervousness and being shy can make us feel foolish. This can happen at any time, from 14 to 40, and is quite normal for everyone. We can work on that condition with our self-esteem and confidence in place. Also, in that desperate moment, take a deep breath and talk more slowly – this will help you to relax.

Being up to date with current affairs is another way of gaining confidence in a group. It will give you information and subjects to talk about, because people often discuss what is happening and how it affects them. Relationships, fashion, politics, and sport will probably be the main topics.

Doing well at school, university or in a job are also ways of increasing your self-esteem. Success breeds success and the approval of family and friends increases your confidence.

One way of gaining more self-esteem is using and giving your friends support. Talk about things that worry all of you. Increase your understanding of how other boys cope with issues and where they get the knowledge to handle growing up – we can't know it all at 14, or ever.

Like it or not, we all need the knowledge, acknowledgment and approval that family and friends can give us, and their help can be invaluable to get through those hard growing up years.

Education is probably the most important influence to your future and your self-esteem. If you can't spell, for instance, you will be defensive when writing or filling in forms, which has a negative influence on self-esteem. This is just one area of education that can affect you, so try and work hard at all subjects. Your success is down to you alone, because no one else can do it for you.

If you don't see school as your way ahead, be sure your alternative is the right one, because if you get it wrong, it could impact on your future and your opportunities.

Whatever you do, be positive – it is one of the single most important factors of success. When you are positive, you can research what you want. Ask questions of family and friends to form the decisions that you are going to have to be positive about.

With the confidence and knowledge you have gained, your ability to analyse the situations and decisions you have to make will naturally be there.

One of those decisions is about how you look – and if you are unsure what your personal style is, look around you – a lot of people are naturally good at seeing what suits them. Books and magazines are another good source of information. Note all the styles; try friends' clothes on and see if they suit you. Your friends will soon tell you if they don't.

You may not get it right straight away, but it will come over time. Like all the features of growing up, it is a steep learning curve; the idea of writing this book is to help shorten that process and lessen your anxiety.

The expression "geek" is often used to describe a bright and sensitive young man, who hides behind big hair, scarves and dull clothes. There is no need to hide behind clothing and hair, unless you feel happy that way. It may be your style, but if it is not, act now and be who you want to be.

When seeking a girlfriend, look for a girl that is your type. If you are a gypsy and the girl you fancy is a princess, it can work, but that is highly unlikely. Try not to look outside your comfort zone – if you do, it will make you feel insecure and it will damage how you feel about your true value. It is not unknown to have a relationship outside your perceived status structure, up or down, but it does have its problems: money, friends, and the way that we speak all have an effect.

Gypsies have a strong family bond and are happy in the company of their own people. Their strength and sense of self is gained by doing what is good for them, and we can learn something from them.

We should all be happy with how we look, but modern society is obsessed with looks and how attractive we are to the opposite sex. The art of feeling good is about looking good and knowing it. If there is anything you want to change about the way you look, if possible, change it.

Plastic surgery has helped millions of people and could help you. Pinning back ears and nose jobs are the most common. Make sure that you research the right clinic and surgeon to do the work. Show the surgeon what you want to change with a sketch of that change. This will show the surgeon that you have thought it through with care and common sense and with a positive view. There have been a lot of mistakes made and faces ruined by unskilled practitioners, so choose your surgeon carefully.

First, be sure that the change you want is for the right reason. You can change your face, but that insecurity you feel inside will still be there. Building your own self-esteem is the first thing you can do before having surgery, and it's far less painful. Building self-esteem can neutralise the ugliest-looking person, because he is confident and knows who he is.

We have all seen the ugly guy with the gorgeous blonde. He has high self-esteem and self-belief, and the blonde is attracted to that. She sees past the looks and sees the man. So surgery should be your last choice.

When we go out looking for a partner or girlfriend, we will often be told, "no thanks" – and some responses will not be so polite. Don't take the rejection personally; it is the normal selection process at work. We cannot be fancied by everyone and it would be unnatural if we were. Girls have similar problems to boys but in reverse – some never get asked out. However, women have lots of advice through magazines and books to sort out the reasons why, but men do not.

Some girls ask out boys, which is good. If it happens to you, go out with her, whether you fancy her or not – it is valuable experience in holding conversation and interaction. Also, by not rejecting her, you have made someone happy, and you never know what may happen!

In the great order of life, **we will be rejected many times,** not just by women, but by employers too. There is always someone brighter than you and more fitted for a particular task. Take heart; you will be able to do things that the brighter or more suited person cannot do. It is said that we are all good at 10 things. What we have to do is recognise them when we do them.

One of the best ways to continue the feel-good factor and self-esteem is to tell yourself many times in your head how good you are, this will help reinforce that self belief, self esteem and respect that we all need. The self-doubts that we have about ourselves seem more believable than the positive views we have. So talk yourself positive; then believe it – you will make it true, because it is true.

CHAPTER 6

Confidence

Confidence is closely linked to your own self-esteem and can be gained from different sources. The primary source of confidence is how you feel about yourself and your self-belief. The young man's job is to strive to become independent and individual, and to build on confidence-gaining activities. In the search to do this, he must try and find the easiest and least stressful way, whether he understands all there is to know or not about his striving to be himself.

This is not an easy job when you have parents telling you what to do and how to behave. This time in your young life is hard to understand, because you do not know where the boundaries are for your independence and who exactly you are.

This will come in time and it is up to you how hard you are going to make it. The teenager who kicks off at his parents all the time is going to find it harder and his confidence will not be improved. Think first about what your parents are asking of you or telling you. Gain from their experience and knowledge – this is the first part of gaining confidence. But still be yourself – you will have your own thoughts and views on items up for discussion.

You can always ask a question if you are not sure of anything. Parents are only too keen to help their child understand the world they are in.

You can gain confidence in your job, or from being at university or college, but still be socially shy and reserved. Shyness is a result of being unsure, or, low self-confidence about the social situation you are in, and not knowing or understanding who and what you are.

The reddening face that happens in the company of women or at tricky social moments is also linked to your confidence and to the experience that you have not yet gained. We all have experienced the red face at some point. Unfortunately, there is no substitute for experience and that is something that we all have to do for ourselves and I hope that this book will help you do that less painfully.

Putting yourself in situations where you can gain social experience is the best form of therapy. Facing up to your inhibitions is the only way to cure them. You will suffer more red faces – some due to lack of experience on a personal level with girls or life in general, but as you get more used to different social situations, the internal embarrassment and red faces you suffer will diminish.

Social awareness and interpersonal skills are qualities that can be learned and are paramount in gaining confidence. Practice is the answer; watch how other people do it, observe the confident person and see what makes him confident. A sense of humour can be a good place to start.

Making people laugh is one of the most attractive traits you can develop, although it is a trait that not everyone can master. A quick wit is necessary if you want to be funny, and it can be one of the 10 things you may be good at, but it is not essential to be funny. Confidence can be gained by being a charmer, and that comes with being at ease with yourself and with the company you are with. When you have built on your self-esteem and are feeling good about yourself, it means that you can then care about others. Charm can be a by-product of caring, because that is how it manifests itself.

When people comment on charm, it's generally because the charmer is interested in the people he is talking to. He asks questions about them, and because of his confidence, he does not have to work at it. The people he is talking to do most of the talking, and the charmer is a good listener – it comes naturally to him. Charm and humour can be a by-product of each other, with confidence being the key.

If you read a lot of books, you will be able to comment on many more different subjects. You can read newspapers that have something sensible to comment on, and this can keep you more informed on current affairs, which enables you to join in conversations about local and world events.

Confidence can be a transient feeling and can come and go with each day but the more you do and the more you know, the more confident you will be in the long term.

Keeping fit is another way of feeling good about you. A healthy body helps with a clear-thinking, healthy mind. Women generally like a well-defined, muscular body, so there is a positive spin off to being fit. The more energy you have, the more things you will want to do, and some young women prefer active men.

Seeking out new friends and hobbies, joining clubs and taking part in sports are excellent ways of gaining confidence. Learning the new skills of a hobby or sport is both satisfying and confidence building.

Do not start something that is outside your mental and physical capabilities. An important part of maintaining your confidence is, knowing your own limits. If you don't like heights, stay off ladders!

Getting to know girls is another way of gaining confidence and this is possibly the most difficult one. This is uncharted territory to the young man starting out on the quest for a girlfriend, and we need a special kind of care and attention skills for that job.

We cannot all have a girlfriend when we want one. We have to go out and make the effort – but don't feel bad if it doesn't happen straight away, enjoy the freedom. When you get a girlfriend, they can become time consuming and expensive.

We all mature at different rates, so gain your confidence and give yourself time to grow into the moment that is right and comfortable for you.

When you are comfortable talking to girls or other social contacts, and feeling good about your place in any conversation, your confidence will have raised to a level that you no longer worry about approaching girls or about your conversation skills.

One way of losing your confidence is falling behind with your school or college work or behind with your living expenses and other bills. This can be a real downer. Seek help if you get behind with your work, or get into debt, before the problem gets out of hand.

There are many things in life that can affect your confidence. One is the verbal abuse or bullying you can get from people at school, college or work, and how you respond to it. Sometimes it can be with anger and abuse of your own.

Anger is a very destructive emotion and can get you into a lot of trouble.

For example, if you make a wrong move in a car or motorbike and the guy in front calls you an idiot, and you leap out of your car and smack him in the mouth, you will end up feeling like a real idiot, especially when the guy you hit calls the police. Not only could you get a criminal record for the assault, you could have damaged your future, confidence, and the way you see yourself and how others see you.

There are some young men who enjoy causing trouble at football matches, and go just to cause trouble and get into fights. The buzz these guys get from this kind of behaviour is not always understood, but there is usually some kind of anger in their past life that causes them to vent their behaviour on society in this way.

Research shows that young men who have been in court and ended up in jail for violent crime do see what a waste of time their hooligan-like behaviour has been. Often, it has taken a prison sentence for them to get a reality check on what they have been doing, and how bad this is for their confidence and general well-being.

If you are one of these unfortunate young men, and find you have the need to be violent, try and talk to someone about it (see help numbers at the back of this book), because when you have a prison record, it can affect your whole future: your job prospects, your social well-being, your self-esteem, and how you feel about yourself.

Reacting to provocation, or causing trouble for the sake of it, can be a very negative emotion, and is mostly done on the spur of the moment, when the action is taken before you have thought through the consequences.

If you can recognise and think through these confidence-destroying minefields, you will be well placed to avoid them, and to limit any damage as you go along. If you can walk away from a possibly dangerous situation, without reacting negatively, this will make you proud of who you are.

Confidence will not come overnight. Being positive and thinking positively is the best way forward. Ask yourself whether an argument is worth winning or a point worth making. If it is not important, then don't bother with it. If you kick off at someone when they do something mad on the road, or down the pub, or anywhere else, the other person will probably retaliate at your response. This is negative and only makes these issues worse – and what have you gained from the confrontation? Nothing!

Therefore, go out there and be confident. Think about what is worth doing and what is good for you, and **be responsible for yourself** in the actions you take. You can be assertive if you don't like a situation you find yourself in, but keep your calm, and talk things through. This will help you gain and maintain your confidence by being a stronger person.

The stronger person you have become, will give you that self respect you deserve, therefore you will be able to show respect for others and their point of view.

CHAPTER 7

Sex and Sexuality - I
Getting prepared

Sex and sexuality are one of the most important parts of being a man, and can define who and what we are. The transition from boy to man is a difficult one, but there is a lot of information that can help make that transition less stressful.

All of the information in this chapter is designed to give you the help and knowledge that you may need to face women less stressfully – and with that edge of know-how to make your progress more enjoyable.

All of the items I have mentioned so far in this book are needed to give you confidence in the task of winning with women, and the skill of attracting them.

It is the most difficult, joyful, and painful of all the things we do when growing up, and to achieve success takes time and practice.

Don't get discouraged if the first girl you talk to does not jump straight into bed with you. This is normal. It does take a lot of practice. Good-looking boys will find it easier, as do good-looking girls. The less attractive guy may have to work harder, but he will be the better man for it, and his victory will be that much sweeter.

My view is that women are mentally and emotionally stronger than men – but luckily for us, they do like and need us, just as we need them.

We tend to give girls the same respect that we give to our mothers before they have earned it. Having too much respect for girls puts you on the back foot straight away. Get girls into perspective, and get them down from that pedestal. Even the most beautiful girls have to go to the toilet like you. Talk to them like you would your sister – with confidence.

If you have got your confidence head on, you are halfway there. Ask them about themselves – it's what they're most interested in! Jobs, hobbies, and music are always good ice-breaker subjects to start with.

Compliment them on their choice of outfit. This is very important to them. They will have spent hours getting ready to make themselves look good. Tell them they look good. This kind of praise is music to their ears. Don't rush the conversation, or seem desperate. This can put a girl off.

They like cool customers, and sometimes a little bit of indifference can work, but it does not work for all girls. If they fancy you, you may then become a challenge. If you are not the best looking boy on the block, you will probably have to work harder at chatting up the girls. This is normal. There are very few good-looking boys and men, so not every girl can have one.

Don't be put off by what seems like an impossible task. A lot of girls are reassured by the ordinary guy – he is the norm, and girls like the norm. They also like excitement, and it is up to you to show that you are capable of exciting her.

A good number of boys choose to dress on the fringe of normal. This will cut down the number of girls that will find them attractive, and could be a bad move. The geek only looks like a geek, because of the way he dresses, and the way he behaves and what he feels about himself. Long, unwashed hair is a turnoff to most girls, but there are a few who do like the dirty look. A good rule of thumb is to maximise your attractiveness to the largest number of women.

The fashion industry is set up to make us all look good. We all have to wear and buy clothes. Buy them wisely. Some items of clothing look good on the hanger, but look hideous on you, so it is important to dress correctly and wear the clothes that you are comfortable in. Dressing well will increase your chances of success with the fairer sex. If in doubt, ask your family, or you could get friends to go shopping with you. Mums and sisters will be only too pleased to go shopping with you. Most women live for a retail therapy session. It's in their genes. Your dad or male friends may give you help in choosing what suits you. However, most men dislike shopping with a vengeance!

One way of looking your best is to smile. Even ugly guys look good when they smile. Pay attention to your teeth. It's no good smiling and trying to be charming with dirty teeth. If there's something wrong with your teeth, get them fixed. They are the first thing that girls will notice when you are trying to chat them up. It will also affect your confidence if you know that you don't look your best when you smile. It may also affect the way you present yourself. Cleaning your teeth will help with fresh breath. It is a good idea to clean your teeth before you go on any girl-pulling night out.

Get your hair done to the fashion of the day, but not to an extreme. Getting it wrong will also cut down the number of women who may fancy you. Seek advice on what suits you. What you do with your hair is important. Being individual with your hair is also important, but it is easy to look an idiot if you get it wrong.

Some men lose their hair very young, and this may cause them some grief, but most of those who are bald look better as they are. It's the comb-over that doesn't do it for women!

You could cut your hair short if you are losing your hair. You will look tougher, and bald men also exude a kind of scent or pheromone that does attract women, so think of the positive: the bald man has something the guy with a full head of hair does not have.

Chatting up girls is a very complicated business. If you have put into place all of the things that I have mentioned before, it will still take practice. Introduce yourself. Talk about anything: ask the girl what her name is, if you do not know it already. You may want to become friends before dating is on the cards. This could be your way of doing things. There are no rules on how you do it. You may want to get to know her and she you, so don't rush any stage of the getting to know you process. Your conversation can become friendlier and more intimate. You can talk about anything, but girls will probably not be interested in car engines and chain-saws.

If you do as much as possible to present yourself in the best possible way, your own style will develop, and so will your personality.

Making girls laugh is possibly the best aphrodisiac, but is not always easy to do if you are self-conscious or nervous. When you have gained confidence and feel at ease, being funny will come naturally to you.

Having gained the attention of the girl you fancy, talk to her about subjects that are of interest to both of you. You could pursue the chance of a meeting or dating again at a place that suits you both.

If a particular woman is not interested, she will soon let you know – if women are not interested, it is difficult to keep their undivided attention. To minimise the chances of rejection, do pay attention to her body language and mood towards you. If it feels wrong, it generally is. But don't ever get put off by rejection. It is normal, and is a part of your development and the learning curve that we all have to go through. If she says yes, gain confidence from that, and then think about how far you want to go with your relationship.

I feel that it is important to develop a relationship with a girl and to spend time getting to know her. Becoming friends and having a good time shows that you are compatible in more ways than one.

CHAPTER 7

Sex and Sexuality - II
Approaching sex

Having sex in a relationship is a development of that good feeling you have together, and is best once you know a person and feel comfortable with them over a reasonable length of time. Sex is possibly the single most intimate thing you can do together, and should be taken seriously and treated with care and respect.

I am not going to tell you how to seduce a girl, or tell you how to do something young men have been doing for millions of years, because there are so many ways to do it. What I can do, is to give you some basic knowledge to help you cope with some of the demands of the modern, better informed, free thinking woman of today.

We all develop our own style, but I can give you some headline hints on what to do to give you clues on progress. You will not seduce a girl who does not want to be seduced. Never rush things with any girlfriend. It may scare her off.

Put your hand gently on the girl's cheek as a pre-kiss lead in. If she leaves your hand there, you can go ahead and kiss her. "Gently" is the key word for any action towards a woman. Putting both hands on her waist is also a gentle move – or try any move of your own that you feel is reassuring to the woman. You don't want her to think that you are forcing the pace.

It is important not to think that seduction happens on the first date. It could be the first date or it could be the 100th date – there is no formula. The girl will soon let you know where she will let you go. Never impose your will on her. This will help to reassure her and ensure that she sets the pace.

Our first sexual encounters when we are young can be clumsy – but if you are better informed in how to go about it, it can be a more pleasurable, if not an expert, experience.

Teenagers generally do not have much choice of where they can go to be alone, but they will always find a way. It could be her place, or your place, or anywhere that is suitable. Wherever you choose, it has to be right for both of you. The more comfortable the place you find to make love, the better it will feel, and the progress will be more natural.

A woman who wants to make love with you is like all your Christmas presents rolled into one, and should be unwrapped carefully. The way you undress her will show her how much you care.

Tearing off all your clothes and hers in a rush may be alright in the movies, but in real life, those who indulge in that kind of passion find it is seldom satisfactory for both partners.

Taking her clothes off slowly will reassure her, and heighten the anticipation for both of you. Remember that she may be shy or embarrassed at showing you her body. Reassure her, tell her how beautiful she is, and kiss her gently.

At every stage of this exploratory process, reassure her: you will also feel nervous and unsure, and also shy at a girl seeing you naked. That is normal: we all have doubts about our manhood when we are young, and if you think your penis has to be 10 inches long, forget it.

Men with large penises have problems finding women who can take 10 inches; the vagina is not made to take that sort of size and would need to take great care not to penetrate too deep, so as not to damage the woman's inside. Man's natural desire to thrust is inhibited, so the man with a 10-inch penis can have his pleasure decreased. He will need to control his natural instinct to thrust, and will have to pace his movements. Although this situation is rare, it can happen.

The average size for the male human penis is about six inches, which means many men have penises that are smaller, and some that are bigger. They say that size doesn't matter. It does matter, but it matters more what you do with it.

When you both have the joy of nakedness, and are enjoying the pleasure of touching each other, you can caress her breasts and lightly squeeze her nipples. You can do this with your fingers or with your tongue, but be careful. The nipple is not the tuning knob of your radio. It is one of a woman's most erogenous zones and should be treated sensitively. You can very lightly grip the nipple between your teeth, and flick it with your tongue, backward and forward. This can be highly erotic for a woman. You can also lightly squeeze her breasts to add to her arousal.

By trying different ways of caressing a woman, you can tell what she likes best by her reaction. Take your clues from your girlfriend's response; she will let you know what she likes best. The most important factor of making love to a woman is to look after her needs. It is easy for men to come to orgasm, but women take a lot more foreplay (sexual arousal before penal penetration), and attention than men. Take pleasure in it – you will feel better about yourself, and your partner will love you for the attention.

Too many men think "knickers off, thrust penis in." That is not the way to go about things: your orgasm will not be as good and she will not even be warmed up. This approach is selfish and self-defeating – your woman will not be happy and she may end up wanting to end the relationship.

Before you embark on penetrative sex, make sure you are protected. You do not want to make your partner pregnant. If you are sixteen the last thing you want is a child and all the problems and expenses that they bring.

There are many sexually transmitted diseases (STDs) that you can contract from sexual intercourse, and care should be taken to prevent you from catching them, so always use a condom.

There are many sexually transmitted diseases that the young man should know about. The one that is in the news quite often is HIV (Human Immunodeficiency Virus). The disease that develops from HIV is AIDS (Acquired Immunodeficiency Syndrome). This can only be transmitted through bodily fluids (semen and blood). Some other diseases that you should know about are chlamydia, gonorrhoea, genital ulcers, trichomonasis, chancroid, urethritis, syphilis, genital herpes, genital warts, pubic lice, and scabies. You can get more information on these diseases on the Internet – or if you are worried about any symptoms you may have in the future, consult your doctor.

When you get to know your partner, you can discuss protection and contraception. If your partner decides to go on the pill, be careful: some girls want to get pregnant. When you trust her, you can then reassess your position about using condoms. The pill is only 98% effective, so to be sure, using a condom as well may be safest.

One of the main complaints by women against men is **premature ejaculation** (reaching orgasm too soon). Although this is normal for young men, or if a man has not had sex for a while, the trigger point can be set to go on entering the vagina or after a few strokes. One way of lowering your trigger point is to masturbate about three to four hours before you think you may have sex. This also takes the urgency out of your foreplay and desire to penetrate her prematurely.

After caressing her breasts, you can move your hands down her body, across her stomach and down between her legs. If you gently stroke the inside of her thighs, this will help to part her legs. This is a natural reaction to your caresses.

A lot of men are unsure of the best place to start when engaging in vaginal foreplay. The clitoris is the most sexual sensitive external part of the female genitalia, and it is in the top centre folds between her legs, and just below her pubic hair. The vaginal passage is just below that.

The clitoris can vary in size, and is generally easy to find. By caressing the fold area gently, the clitoris will enlarge slightly. Use a very light touch when caressing the clitoris, because you can put a woman off if you use a too hard a pressure, or are too rough. When your caresses are successful, the effect will be noticeable by your partner's reaction of heightened excitement.

Women gain a lot of pleasure from clitoral stimulation, and you could ask her where is best to touch for her. When your girlfriend is ready for penetration, you will be able to judge by her excitement, or she may even say that she is ready.

You can insert one or two fingers into the vagina for further stimulation, stroking in and out gently, with a slight pressure to the front. Inside the vagina, about two inches in at the front, is possibly the most sensitive and erotic zone of a woman's body. The more attention you pay to these areas during foreplay, the more chance there is of her achieving a climax with you during penetration.

She may want to hold your penis at this stage. If she is shy, she may not. You can encourage her to do so as part of your approach to penetration. There are no set rules of how long foreplay should take – only practice will make you confident in this area, as with all aspects of making love.

It may be a good idea to proceed slowly in all areas of foreplay, and not to rush any part. Although you are excited, do try and resist the rush to intercourse. Take your time – it will be worth it.

There never seems to be a good time to apply a condom. You can, if you are not careful, lose that special moment – but you should try to do it. The sooner you apply a condom, the better. There is a risk of pregnancy if penetration takes place before you put on a condom: even if you do not ejaculate, the fluid your penis discharges can have live sperm in it.

You could lie back and put it on before trying penetration, or you could get your partner to do it. This may help to take away any embarrassment and you could even have a laugh about it. You could also practice this in the privacy of your own bedroom to perfect it.

When you first try penetration, this can be the most awkward and potentially the most embarrassing for you both. Climb between your partner's legs with your knees level with hers, and take your weight with one hand level with her breasts, near her underarm. With your other hand, hold your penis and guide it into the vagina, lowering your body toward your partner. You can caress the clitoral area carefully with the end of your penis. This will help lubricate, and ease entry to her vagina.

Take the penetration slowly. It can take three or four or more short strokes to gain full-length entry, and it can be painful for a girl the first time or if rushed. Be sensitive at all times to your partner's feelings. She is not a machine, and needs care and consideration.

Take things slowly. Put most of your weight on your elbows or hands, on either side of your partner. Long, slow strokes are a good way to start. If the desire to come is there, you could stop for a few minutes to give you time to recover your control. You could kiss and caress her again during this slow-down. If you think you both feel ready, your own feelings and your partner's will take you through the rest to climax.

There is no set time for how long sex should last, but when you are starting out, it probably will not last that long. The joy of being young is that your recovery rate from coming is quite fast, and you can perform the sex act again soon after the first time, sometimes with a better result.

After making love, it is good to still be attentive. Rolling over and falling asleep is not what a woman wants. **Cuddle her** and let her rest her head on your chest. Those "after" moments will mean a lot.

When you are more relaxed and practiced about making love, you could try holding on to delay your orgasm. This will enable your partner to orgasm first. This is not always easy to do, and may need a little practice. You can try in the privacy of your bathroom, when you go to have a pee, to stop the flow halfway through. This will show you which muscles you have to use during sex to prevent orgasm when you have the desire to climax. Stop and tense those muscles at the base of your penis and rectum that you felt when stopping having a pee. It may take a little time to get it right, but it will be worth it.

There are other ways of delaying your orgasm, like inducing some kind of pain to your penis as a distraction, or thinking of something else to lower your desire to come. The longer you can hang on to your climax, the better your orgasm, and your partner will think more of you after her extended orgasms.

As you become more skilled, your performance and abilities will increase. Your partner will start to get used to you, and learn to trust your methods of love-making. You can then discuss what each other's preferences are.

There are lots of variations to sex, and the sex act. My aim is to get you past those first nerve-racking stages of experience that we all have to go through. Don't worry about your performance when making love, because this can cause anxiety. We all have to learn at some point, but if we take care of our partners, we are half way there.

Enjoy your learning time, and enjoy finding out all the different ways and things there are to know about sex.

Do you think you're gay?

If you have doubts about your sexuality, and think that you may be gay, there are many ways that you can make sure that this is right for you. It is not unusual for young men to be confused about their sexuality, so give it time – and if you are sure, pursue your path with caution. As with any sexual relationship, there are health risks to take into account, HIV being the most common.

For more information, there are gay magazines, books, clubs, videos, CDs, the Internet and friends who could possibly be of help to you.

Research your feelings inside yourself and out there in society to make sure this is the right decision for you. This process will help you define how you feel and focus on the issue and the reality of what homosexuality is. Make sure that your feelings of being gay are right. If you want to come out about your sexuality, you have a right to do that, as well.

All of the feelings that heterosexual boys feel, gay boys will also feel – if not more so. The same insecurities and self-doubts will be there, plus the feeling of being different. This, too, is normal and OK.

If there is anything that bothers you about any of these subjects, talk to someone you trust, or use help lines, libraries, and magazines: they are all there to help you. (There are also some numbers for your help at the back of this book).

Chapter 8

Cry For Help

It is sometimes difficult for teenagers to talk about thoughts and issues that worry them, and are a problem to them. Parents sometimes seem to be the last people that a teenager could confide in, because of embarrassment about the subject, or a feeling that their parents would not understand.

If you are suffering from any kind of stress or worries, you should try to talk about what is causing the feelings you are having. There is nothing to be gained from keeping a problem inside and keeping them to yourself. The biggest and strongest men still have problems, and have a need to share them with someone who cares.

Women are generally good listeners, and your mother is probably your first choice, but if the subject is too sensitive, anyone that you trust will do. Trust is the most important factor in who you choose to share your situation with.

If the issue is so embarrassing to you that you cannot share it with your mother, there are many ways of getting information and help. Help lines, books, the Internet, your doctor, or a counsellor could help.

Some schools have an in-house counsellor or trained teacher who is there to help you, so ask a member of staff. If you do not feel safe doing that, ask a friend if they know of someone you can talk to in confidence.

A private counsellor is another way of seeking help that is open to you, but this will cost you money, so exhaust all other avenues first.

There is no shame in admitting that you may have a problem and find issues difficult to cope with. No one goes through life without that feeling at some point in time. However, the ability to talk about your problems is the first step to solving them. The old saying that a problem shared is a problem halved is very true, but choose carefully who you share your worries with.

There are many issues that can concern a young man, which you may think are only suffered by you. This is a normal feeling. These feelings, thoughts, and worries about ourselves can be untruths about ourselves that we internally think or verbalise, which can cause us a lot of stress. If you can talk about these feelings, you will find that you are not alone in how you feel and that what you are feeling is normal.

Young men can worry about their height, the size of their penis, being too fat or too thin, being bullied, drugs and alcohol, fear of dying or fear of someone they love dying, or just trying to keep up with the boys, who seem to have all the male attributes that a man should have.

All these thoughts are normal. There is no problem or feeling in this world that has not been felt before. Anxiety is possibly the most common feeling that young people tend to live with. Some levels of anxiety or stress are needed to get us up and motivated, but if it is at a level that is intolerable, then seek help. There is a higher rate of suicide among young men, because they feel it is not manly to have feelings, or feel that they are unable to cope, and would be best off out of it.

Some boys and girls run away from home to get out of the place that is causing their anxiety. If you feel like this, think before you move out. The world out there is a very dangerous place, and the decision to move out should be thought through carefully.

The streets of London are a common place for kids to go. If you are thinking of going there, be aware: it is crowded and dangerous, and you may fall victim to sex crime gangs or paedophiles that prey on young children. You could get mugged and have the important items that you have bought with you stolen. This could ruin your chances of survival.

The streets of any city are no place for a child or unprotected young adult. Therefore, it is important that you try and talk to someone about why you want to run away. That talk could change your feelings about what is hurting you, and that could save you a lot of suffering.

Some serious issues that are hard to cope with are abuse and bullying, so do not suffer in silence, these are serious events and need to be resolved.

Tell someone about it. Schools and colleges do take this problem seriously, and will act to stop it.

If your parents split up, this, too, can cause anxiety and feelings of guilt. You may worry that it is some way your fault. This is a normal feeling for you or your siblings to feel. When a family situation changes, you should talk to someone to help you understand that change, and to cope with your feelings about it.

Young people are given a lot of information on drugs that is in contrast to what is the reality. There is no such thing as a harmless drug. Some kill, some can become addictive, and some result in mental health problems. If you have questions or worries about a drug problem, ask the experts.

There are times in a young man's life when he has worries and issues where he feels that no one can understand him or what he is suffering. These feelings are common and should not be ignored, as they can lead to depression, and sometimes this also can lead to the desire to kill oneself.

These feelings young men have are intense and meaningful, and need to be expressed, and understood. The feeling of, **"it would be useless to talk"** is not uncommon. **"No one understands how I feel"** is another common feeling. If you feel this way, you are not alone, so do try talking – it does help.

Another feeling that is hard to talk about, but should not be ignored, is anger. This is a very destructive emotion and can come from the most unlikely places.

When a young man's father or mother dies suddenly, after the sadness, comes the feeling of anger. The feeling of not understanding what has happened is coupled with that of being unable to see his future without the support of the person who has died. The feeling of abandonment is not uncommon.

When a parent remarries, and you find it hard to get on with your new step mum or dad, you can get angry at being told what to do by someone who is not your parent.

You could have new step-siblings whom you cannot accept or do not get on with.

You may be frustrated by not being able to achieve at school, or work, not feeling good enough at what you are trying to do, and not being able to do it well. Low self-esteem can make you angry, and resentful of other boys who seem to be getting on better than you.

All these feelings are normal, but if you still feel angry, talk about that anger with people who will understand you, and are ready to listen. If you cannot talk to your parents, or family, try talking to a family counsellor, this is a good place for this kind of help.

Phone help lines are also there to help you, no matter what the subject is, and this is a far less expensive way to get help than going to a counsellor. The most important feature of help lines is that they are confidential. The person you are talking to does not know you – therefore, you are anonymous. This will help you to talk freely about any problems or any feelings you may have, thus helping to reduce your anxiety.

There are courses in anger management, and if you feel that you are suffering any of these symptoms, try talking to someone to resolve your anger: being short-tempered, feeling angry and not knowing why, causing arguments for no reason with family and friends, the desire to be violent to others just for fun, or just angry thoughts. If you feel any of these things and think an anger management course could help you, do try it, before your anger gets you into trouble.

There are many young men who get in trouble with the law because their anger has spilled over into inappropriate behaviour or activities and that has harmed their future. This is due to issues and feelings of frustration and anger, at being misunderstood and let down.

Another important situation that young men have to handle is **being dumped by a girlfriend.** This is possibly one of the most distressing and ego-shattering events to face young men, and the same feeling is felt by every man of any age at some point in his life. The loss of someone you love, and the feeling that she could be with another man can be totally consuming, and you can see no way ahead without that person.

All of these feelings are intense and hard to cope with, but it is how you handle the loss that is important. Crying is a good way to help release pent-up feelings. Talking to family and friends is another. But some young men feel that self-harming is another way to cope with the pain. Thoughts of killing yourself are sometimes another way of getting rid of the **desperate, painful feelings of rejection.**

All of these feelings are normal, but it is how we seek to recover from them that is important. Seeking help is the first stage, and talking, help lines and counselling could be the starting point. All of these methods do take a lot of courage, but are better than harming yourself in some way.

You will be surprised at how many people are out there to assist and help you at such a hard time. We all need help at some point in our lives, no matter how old we are, so do not be afraid to ask for what you need. It takes courage and strength to ask for that help.

Chapter 9

Work

Finding or deciding what you want to do to earn a living is a hard one for young men and women. A lack of worldly experience can leave them in a confused state about what to do. The most important factor is that whatever you decide, **it should be a job that you will enjoy**. You could be at work for more than 40 years, and if you are in a job you hate, it will seem like 80 years.

When thinking about your choice, think about what subjects you like and what you are good at. This will give you ideas for jobs.

Research your job through directories, libraries, the Internet and books to maximise your choices. Find out as much as you can about the jobs you want to investigate. Find companies that do the kind of work you like. Companies are always looking for young talent, so talk to them, phone them, or knock on their door. Do what you have to. It may seem daunting, but do not let it put you off. It is important to you that you get it right. If it does seem too daunting, try to think of other ways to achieve your goals.

When you have made your choice, you need to get the information together and go through it so that you can make an informed and valid selection. Then you need to get the education that matches the job. University is one route, and this will give you the building blocks of a good career. The better the degree you get, the better your chances in that career. Doctor, accountant, scientist, mathematician, or psychiatrists are just a few of the careers that you can choose. They all need further qualification after your first degree, and some need that crucial on the job training that only experience can give you.

Jobs within the police, prison, ambulance and fire services all need on the job training after your initial training.

The army is another positive career choice. Many trades and occupations can be gained while serving as a soldier. You could also train as an officer if you have the right qualifications and character qualities. There is no limit to what you can achieve in the army if you put the effort in to the field that you choose to follow.

There is however downside to the army: you can get shot at, and get killed. If this is a concern, weigh up the odds relative to civilian life, where your local high street is also a dangerous place. Think it through, and talk to your family about all the aspects of army life. Talk to the army. Research the dangers, compared to the great life experience you will receive in the army. If you are unsure, then the army is probably not for you.

Engineers, car mechanics, and all of the building trades also need on the job training with college courses to gain the relevant qualifications to do the job properly.

These examples are just a few, but when you make your choice, make sure that it is within your capabilities. There is no value in stepping out of your comfort zone and struggling – we cannot all be brain surgeons.

If you do want to be a brain surgeon badly enough, and are capable, you will work hard to get there.

There are some jobs that need no formal training. The entrepreneur, for instance, is a law unto himself. He has that special something that enables him to make money where we would not. He will see that business opportunity that will enable him to build up a company – sometimes to unbelievable dimensions. Richard Branson is a good example of this.

Although we all think that we can be an entrepreneur, it can be fraught with danger: business opportunities can go wrong and lose money, so seek advice if you have a good idea. If you have invented a product, make sure that your idea is protected before talking about it. The Patent Office website will have information on what you need to do to protect your idea.

When you embark on a job, there is no guarantee that you will have that job for life, but take heart – you can train for another career at any time in your life. There is no age limit to success. So if a job takes your fancy, go for it, if that is what you want.

There are education courses throughout the country at colleges and universities, and online for home study. These courses can cost money, but are not beyond the reach of most people who want to get on.

Some companies may give you financial help for training, if you have proved yourself capable and a hard worker.

The fundamental reason for going to work is to earn money, so research the pay levels for the job you have chosen.

Take all the evidence into account: money, workload, qualifications, job satisfaction, stress levels, and most importantly, whether you like doing the job you have chosen. If all looks good, go for it.

Do remember when studying or learning a new job, that it is hard to achieve all your goals the first time around. There is no such thing as failure, only learning curves to success. Gain experience from things that do not work out, and ask yourself the reason why you did not achieve your goal on that challenge. You can always try again, change course, change job. It is always up to you – just choose your change with more experience, information and care.

CHAPTER 10

Entertainment

One of the most important parts of being young is having fun, so it is important that you know how to do it safely.

There are many things to do and going to the pub is probably the easiest and most common. Having a drink with your mates is a natural thing to do. The chance to interact with your friends and make new ones is what being young is all about.

It is a good place to practice your interpersonal skills and social awareness. Be aware of your surroundings, learn from other people, see how they behave and see what works. Social skills are important in everything you do.

Playing snooker, bar billiards or darts are all good ways of interacting with friends and having a good time.

There is a down side to drinking alcohol in large quantities, because it is not good for you. Although it can make you feel good in moderation, if done to excess, it can become a habit that you can no longer control.

If your drinking does get out of control, seek help, or try and control it. There are serious health risks to alco-

hol abuse. New studies show that binge drinking is causing an increase in kidney and liver disease and failure, in
the young of both sexes.

No doubt you will get drunk at some point, and it
seems to be something that kids have to do. It's painful
for the head and you can be violently sick. When you
have drunk too much, you can also fall asleep and be
sick, and there is a great danger of choking on your
vomit. Try not to mix your drinks – doing so to excess
can lead to you ending up in hospital having your stomach pumped.

Going out to clubs is another thing that you will do
when young. It has the excitement of the music and
dancing and you can meet girls there, so it has to be
good. It is a brilliant way to let off steam and have fun.

The bad news is that drinks in clubs are usually
expensive, so try and find some way of not buying drinks
in the club, or limit the number that you buy.

If the music is too loud, it can damage your hearing in
later life, so take care.

You must also be aware of the drug culture in clubs. You
can be offered drugs, and you do not know what they
are, and some can kill. To make sure of your own safety,
try to refuse them, although it is hard to do with your
friends around. Be strong – do what you want to do.
Looking after your drink is important, there have been
cases of them being spiked (drugged). This is a particular concern to girls.

Getting yourself home at two or three in the morning
after clubbing can also be a testing time when you are
drunk. Getting involved in fights, falling under cars in

the street, or falling off the platform of a train station while waiting for a train are all ways you can get injured, or in some cases, killed.

Be aware of all of these situations when going home after a fun night out, because hundreds of young people die each year due to accidents while drunk.

Never drink and drive. If you have an accident while driving and kill someone, you will go to jail and that is not a fun place. You will also have to live with the guilt of having caused the death of someone for the rest of your life. Instead, walk home carefully, or get a taxi.

All of these things are avoidable if you know your limits on alcohol intake – and this you can find out in a safe way, at home or with friends down the pub.

I know that I am pointing out some of the negative parts of having fun, but if I can tell you the good and the bad, then you can make your choices from an informed standpoint.

Going to see a film at the cinema is a relaxing way to be entertained. You can go with whom you like and it is quite harmless, although horror movies can disturb a good night's sleep.

One of the drawbacks of going to the cinema are that you will pay high prices for drinks, sweets, popcorn, and ice cream, so go prepared with you own food stuff. It is also a place where you can lose your property. Things fall out of your pocket without you noticing, like mobile phones or money. All I can suggest is that you be more aware of where you put your property.

Going to the theatre is a good form of entertainment. There is no limit to subject matter in plays and musicals.

London and New York are possibly the best places in the world for theatre because of the quality of production. Italy and Vienna are good places for opera, and both have their own style.

However, with that quality comes a price tag. It is not cheap to be entertained in London. Apart from the theatre ticket price, the cost of getting to the city and possibly eating out, too, is expensive. Research your night out in town. It is a fun place, and you can enjoy just looking around and getting to know the place.

There are many provincial theatres which have good programmes, and some West End productions go on tour, so keep your eye out in the local and national media for information, if there is something you wish to see. If you are into drama, you can also get involved yourself in local theatre clubs.

Comedy theatre is a specialist form of entertainment and is extremely popular. Comedy workshops and festivals promote the best performers. The press and media advertise these events, such as the Edinburgh Festival, for example.

Going to see sport is another way of entertaining yourself. Football is the most popular sport, and local teams have a lot to offer their fans. The big teams like Manchester United and Chelsea charge a large entry fee to watch their games and if you are young, it will take a good chunk out of your money.

There is always the television, where you can watch your team play if you are prioritising where you spend your money, but you will not feel the atmosphere or perhaps see your team when you want to, due to television schedules.

Other sports to watch or take part in are rugby, hockey, badminton, horse riding, show jumping, polo, skiing, squash, flying, motor bike and car racing, banger racing, off road and track biking and hang gliding. Sports centres and the relevant clubs are the best places for information. You can find their contact details in the Yellow Pages.

All of these sports are open to everyone to be involved in, so pursue them if you are interested enough. Taking part will give you another way of learning more about yourself and the things you like to do. There is always a possibility of another career path in sport.

Art, writing, photography, family history, and travel are some other hobbies that can entertain you, although they are not activities you can always do in a collective way, to enable you to interact with others. There are generally clubs and art workshops where you can exchange ideas and talk through what is going on in your field.

Computer games are another way of entertain yourself, but this can be very isolating for those of a reclusive nature. When you are young, you need to interact with your friends to gain those important interpersonal skills, so try and limit the time you spend on your computer.

MSN and Facebook are good way of keeping in touch with your friends, and you can spend many hours chatting. However, this, too, can become isolating and will not do anything for your spelling and speech!

There is an enormous range of subjects you can study at evening classes. You may not automatically think of an educational establishment as entertainment, but there are many things you can learn about that can grow into hobbies, or even jobs. Family history, creative writing, car maintenance, and languages are just examples of classes that could fit your interest. You can get lists of subjects to study from your local college, or library, who normally print a prospectus, for your information.

These courses do cost money, but it can be money well spent by the value of the course and the people you can meet.

Entertaining yourself is the one thing you can do where you completely choose what you do. It will be a part of your self-expression and the development of your personality. If we have fun, this helps us give balance to our lives. If you just do work, you will become tired and may become depressed.

Entertainment is a very important part of our lives and needs to be developed as much as our education. It helps to make us a more rounded and balanced person.

CHAPTER 11

Holidays

Taking holidays is one of the most enjoyable things we do and they have to be sourced carefully, as the choices seem to be endless of things to do and places to go.

If you are conserving cash, camping is one of the cheapest ways of taking a break, and it can be lots of fun. There are many camp sites that you can choose from around this country and abroad.

The major sites are on the coast and at particular places of interest, and these can be found in camping magazines and holiday brochures. If you want to seek out the sites where you can get back to nature and cook by fire, there are specialist farms and estates that do allow this, but they are getting harder and harder to find.

There has been some land law reform to allow **"wild camping,"** as it is called. This means pitching your tent when hiking, wherever you want. Setting up your tent in wild areas in Scotland is now allowed if a light tent is used for two or three nights only, taking care of all the environmental issues. Wild camping is not generally allowed in England and Wales, particularly on new open access land. The *Dartmoor Commons Act 1985* permits wild camping, providing that you choose your tent site carefully. Don't pitch your tent on farmland, enclosed moorland, or within 100 metres of the highway. Always steer clear of archaeological and other specialist sites. The Lake District and National Trust only allow wild camping in areas 450m above sea level, as long as there are only two campers staying for no more than one night. Wild camping is generally only legal with permission of the land owner.

When camping abroad, always check the local laws and rules. It will save you a lot of grief with foreign authorities. The Internet is an easy source of information for all your needs.

You can be very upfront and ask a local farmer if you can use a free field to pitch your tent. Do seek permission if you want to light a fire.

Choosing a spot to pitch your tent is important – for example, an area shielded from the wind and on reasonably high ground. It's no good pitching your tent on a riverbank – if it rains during the night, you will get washed away. It would not be much fun at four o'clock in the morning trying to take down your tent in the dark with the river around your feet. Keep away from livestock and anywhere that could be a danger to you or to others.

If you are allowed to light a fire, there are certain rules you have to observe. You have to choose a place where there is no chance of the fire spreading to any property or to anything that can cause damage or be a danger to livestock, to you, or anyone else. In dry grassy areas or pine forests, for example, fires can travel through undergrowth undetected. Always check that you are allowed to light a fire.

The best way is to pick a spot away from your tent, preferably downwind, and dig out a turf 400mm x 600mm that is free of any material other than soil. Put this turf to one side, then dig down another 50mm and pile the dirt at the end of the fire space that you have just dug. This can be used as an emergency fire extinguisher by throwing handfuls of dirt on the fire if it gets out of control.

You will need a small hand axe to fashion two folk supports to push into the ground on either side of the fire, to help support your cooking Billy can or pot.

You will need some dry kindling, like straw or dead dry grass, to start your fire, and gradually add larger pieces of dead dry wood to keep it going. Unless you are an expert like Ray Mears, you will need a box of matches or a lighter. If you are into the outdoor life, Ray Mears's book *Bush Craft* would be very useful to you, and I do recommend it – it is a very good read.

You will also need to dig a latrine. This, too, should be some way from the tent site – and downwind and in a private position if possible. Remove turf about 300mm square. Then dig a hole 300mm deep, putting the soil in a heap at the back of the latrine site. This is so the site cannot be disturbed by animals when you have covered up your latrine. A small amount of the soil can be used every time the latrine is used. This will stop any smell or contamination by flies.

It is good manners to leave the site as clean and tidy as you found it. You can put the ashes from the fire onto a compost heap or down the latrine hole, or another spot suggested by the farmer. Put the dirt back into the fire hole and tread it down as flat as possible, then replace the turf, tapping it gently with the back of your spade. Repeat the same process for the latrine, making sure that all is clean and tidy.

Remove all your belongings to your vehicle. When the site is clear, find some bushy twigs and brush over the fire and latrine areas. This will raise the flattened grass and help return the area back to how you found it.

Caravanning is another inexpensive way to spend time away, especially if you are going in a group. This means that you can share the cost of the van and site rental, and there are sites all over the world. These sites are generally accessible by all the main services – road, rail and air – but do check these details.

You can find these sites in brochures and in caravan club literature. The Internet is another good source of information. These sites are generally well equipped with water and electric power points at pitch sites. Also, there are often good toilet and washing facilities, but do check each site you are interested in going to.

You can tow your own caravan if you are legally able, but do take care – caravans are very difficult to handle at speed and you will need good training and experience to do so safely.

Another good holiday that young men find a lot of fun is travelling on **canal narrow boats**. They are reasonably easy to handle and with the speed limit at four miles per hour, it is a good way to de-stress after study or exams.

There are certain rules to observe on the canal, but nothing that common sense cannot handle. The rules will be given to you on the receipt of your boat. These are instructions on how to behave on the canal, and also take safety issues into account, because there are many areas where you can get into trouble.

Working the locks, which allows your boat, to rise and fall to different land and water levels is quite simple, but needs a bit of energy and effort. Locks are also very deep, so this is no place to mess about. Non-slip footwear should be worn at all times.

Lifejackets are also a good idea. It may not seem cool, but drowning is not cool either.

You can hire boats with up to eight berths, which is a good number for friends to get away. It is a good idea to run the trip with a kitty of equal shares, as paying for items separately can become unfair and cause disagreements. Food, fuel and the cost of any other items you may need are shared fairly.

The same rules apply as living in a flat or house: it is better to know the people you go on holiday with, so that you can cut the reasons for arguments and confrontations to a minimum.

The canal routes are all over the country and meander through some of England's most beautiful countryside. Many are close to historical cities and centres of activity. Information and maps can be obtained from the *Inland Waterways Authority*, or holiday companies who arrange fun boating hire holidays. The Internet is also another good place for information.

Skiing is a good healthy holiday and can be done in any size of group. You will more than likely stay in a chalet and live in close proximity to your group.

The chalets are usually run by families or gap year students who love skiing, and they will cook and clean for you and then enjoy the rest of their daylight hours skiing. The quality of cooking can vary, but generally, it is quite good.

The difference to a boating holiday is that it is quite likely you are not all the same standard and will choose to go off to different slopes to suit your level, so you will not be in close company 24-7. This will assist with you not getting on each other's nerves.

In contrast to camping and caravanning, skiing is not a cheap holiday – from the minute that you step onto a train, boat or plane, you are paying ski prices. But it is a lot of fun – not only the skiing but also the nightlife or après-ski.

If you go by train to Europe, the fun can start at the outset of your journey. You can step onto the Eurostar train at St Pancras station in London, and head for Europe through the tunnel to France. This can be some of the best time away. The picnic atmosphere, accompanied with a beer or Champagne, depending on your pocket, can add to your pleasure. It is a wonderful experience to travel at high speed through France to your destination in comfort – and ideal for groups of young men on an adventure.

There are many skiing centres throughout Europe: in France, Spain, Austria, Italy Germany, and Switzerland. Many old Eastern bloc countries are also opening ski resorts of good quality, so check them all out.

French resorts are possibly one of the most crowded and ill mannered in Europe. Pushing and shoving is commonplace on ski lifts and slope queuing.

America and Canada are also good venues for skiing. It may cost you a bit more to get there, but it is not so crowded and bad manners are not allowed, so there is no pushing in the queues. Aspen in Colorado is a very popular place in the US, as are Banff and Whistler in Canada.

The costs of skiing can vary. If you are a beginner, you will need lessons. You will also need to hire your boots and skis. When being fitted for boots, make sure they are the right size, because if they are not, you are in for very sore feet.

It may be better as a beginner to try short skis, as these are easier to handle. The hire company generally give you skis relative to your height, but do ask for a shorter pair – you can always change them if they do not suit you.

You can buy all your clothing in the UK, including thermals, socks, jackets and salopettes. All of this clothing can also be hired, but it could be used for other things, such as trekking, walking or for any other activity where you need warm clothing, so it may be cost effective to buy.

You can also buy skis in most big cities or resorts in any country, but do make sure you like them first, because skis and boots are expensive.

All of the world's ski resorts have information on the Internet or in ski holiday brochures, so choose wisely. By doing your homework and shopping around for the best deals, you can save a lot of money.

Sun-based holidays are well served by the Spanish. The beaches and resorts are generally of good quality and will give the sun worshipper all that he needs.

The first hazard is the sun itself. If you do not use a sun block, you will burn. This could lead to skin cancer, so take care of yourself.

If you are only going on holiday for the sun, then I see no point on going any further than you need. It is the same sun, after all, so don't waste your money. There are some good resorts in the UK, and on a good sunny year, you will not find better anywhere in the world. There is no guarantee of the weather in the UK, but the choice is yours.

If you do choose any other country, try and get involved with the local culture – you will meet some good people and have a much better time.

It is always useful to learn some of the language of the country you are going to. This will pay dividends on how much you get out of your holiday, as being able to interact with the locals is a priceless experience.

Adventure holidays are becoming more popular, and it doesn't matter what age you are. Check out Africa, the Middle East, China, India, Mongolia, mountain trekking in the Alps or in the Andes; touring South America, Australia, Canada, the USA, or anywhere else you can see that a company has an organised trip arranged.

You will find that these trips are in small groups, possibly eight to 20 people, and escorted by guides, as well as sometimes by armed guards, for security and your safety, because some of these destinations can be dangerous.

These holidays can be found in the holiday section of the national press, and also in specialist holiday company brochures and on the Internet.

Research your holiday carefully, so you know what you are getting and letting yourself in for. Check the company running the holiday you have chosen to see that it has been established for some time and has a proven track record. Make sure that it is ABTA bonded for your protection. Try to get some satisfied customer feedback and find out what the holidays are like, as this can help you to make an informed choice about your trip. Internet sites such as Trip Advisor give feedback on all sorts of destinations.

If danger and discomfort is not your thing, think carefully: some of these trips have a camping and sleeping rough as part of the experience. It would not be fair on the other members of your group to have to put up with you whinging about how you did not expect it to be so rough or dangerous. There can be some discomfort above the norm on some of these types of holidays, so research carefully.

Holidays with education and aid working as the focus are also available. Perhaps holiday is the wrong word for this type of trip, but you can get a once in a lifetime experience. The interaction with your fellow workers, students and the people you are there to assist can be personally rewarding, which can be priceless.

This, too, can assist in your life experiences, self-esteem, and confidence-building.

Some charities run field trips to help in deprived parts of the world, doing all kinds of work and giving valuable experience to the students involved.

Colleges, universities and charities are the starting point for information and guidance for your safety. Some large companies also sponsor these kinds of field trips or gap year experiences.

These types of trip are specialised, and you will have to search for and research your options, and understand the full implications of what you want to do with your educational holiday experience. Some of these educational holidays also have a level of danger and a "roughing it" element to them, so do your homework.

Backpacking is one of the most popular ways for young people to see the world for themselves. Without the control of adults, the freedom it can give you can be absolute.

There are many permutations as to the first stop, but Singapore or Bangkok to the east, or New York going west, seem to be high on the list.

You can buy a complete package with your travel arrangements. Some backpackers find that it is better to buy their next travel ticket, when needed. This is to maintain flexibility in days spent in places of interest or the desire to work in and learn more about the language and customs of that city, town or country.

This will impact on the cost, so it has to be your comfort zone decision, do what you are happy with.

The hostel network around the world is extensive. The costs are low and affordable, but the amenities are no frills and basic. The amenities are generally fit for their purpose and are reasonably clean and tidy; bedrooms are mostly shared, with basic washing facilities. Do check out the hostels you intend to use, including the cost, so that you can plan sleeping arrangements and availability and the amount of money you will need for your time away.

Do take care of all your personal property, as people have had cameras and other items stolen from hostels. It may be an idea to download any pictures that you have taken on your trip at an Internet café as you go along, so that if your camera is stolen or lost, you will not lose all of your pictures.

It is very important that you **plan your journey carefully**. It may seem easy enough to get to your first destination and to work it out from there, but unfamiliarity with your surroundings in a new country and city can reduce your confidence and may put you in danger of falling prey to unscrupulous people, such as drug traffickers.

There are some taxi drivers, rickshaw runners and people who are at airports for the sole purpose of enlisting young people into crime and other activities, so be aware of whom you are talking to and accept help or lifts from to reduce the risks as much as possible.

Do not take any packages through customs or anywhere else for someone you do not know. There have been many cases in the press about young people being imprisoned for taking drugs through customs in packets they knew nothing about.

This kind of activity can carry the death penalty in some countries, so take care.

If you plan to travel through first world and third world countries, make sure you understand the difference in cultures, as this will be useful and could keep you out of trouble. It's a massive leap from life in Hamburg, Germany to Delhi in India. Research your centres of interest well for your own safety.

Plan your route and work out how much money you will need. Find out where you will be staying and use transport to your hostel that has a registered ID with the local authorities. Taxis or buses do generally have markings that denote officially recognised permits.

Always try and travel in pairs or groups, as there is much more safety in numbers, and criminals will be less likely to take advantage of two people who are a support for each other.

Not everyone is a criminal, and you will find that most people you meet are helpful and friendly – just be aware when you put your trust in someone.

Your personal security is also important. Talk to your bank to see which is the best way to access your money and the best way to carry it on your person – you want to eliminate the chances of being mugged. One suggestion is a card belt under your clothes, close to your skin. This enables you to notice if anyone is tampering with your belt and also prevents a potential mugger from gaining easy access to your property.

Keep a photocopy of the picture page of your passport in your card belt and on your email; this will save you from a lot of hassle if you are unlucky enough to lose the real thing. You will still have to go to your country's embassy or consulate to get a replacement. There are procedures in place for this eventuality, but this still may take some time.

Plan what you will need in the way of clothes, as the lighter you travel, the easier it is to get around. One back packer I spoke to suggested using the K.I.S.S method:

"Keep it simple, stupid"

Take into account the varied weather conditions that you will encounter and be clear in your mind where you are going, because any change will cost you money in buying extra clothes to suit the weather changes you may encounter.

Sturdy, comfortable walking boots or shoes are one of the most important items, as is a good waterproof rucksack and light-weight raincoat or cape. Being dry and comfortable will make a lot of difference to your confidence and well being, as well as to how you feel you are coping with the natural stresses of being on your own, without the back-up of your parents.

The choice of clothing is yours alone, but bear in mind that you have to carry it, so think it through and discuss it with the people you are going with – there may be items you can share to save weight. Talk to people who have been backpacking already to gain their knowledge and experience.

Researching the places you intend to visit is very important, and being familiar with the layout of a city or town you visit will give you an edge. When faced with finding your hostel or place you wish to visit, that all-important knowledge of where you are will be priceless.

It may be an idea to get map printouts from the Internet of cities or sites of interest, as full maps will become cumbersome. These page maps could be discarded as you move on to your next destination. There are also Internet sites around the world where you can get this information.

It may be a good idea to keep a diary of your journey and record any information you have put on your map page. This, too, can be done online. Either way will give you an historical overview of your trip when you get home, which may help you with any future use to which you put this good life experience.

List of useful items to take with you

Basic medical kit
Basic wash kit (soap, tooth brush
& paste, sun cream!!!)

Swiss army knife
Trousers
Shorts
T shirts
Long shirt
Waterproofs

Flip flops (Personal choice)

Whatever holiday you choose, do your homework to maximise your enjoyment and your safety – it will be worth it.

CHAPTER 12

Fashion

The way you look and dress is one of the most important statements you can make about how you are perceived by other people. Therefore, choosing your style and the clothes that you wear is important in how you want to present yourself.

If your choice of style works best for you and gives you the confidence and self-esteem you need, then you are OK, but if you are not sure about what your style is, ask others for their opinion. People see you as you are; not how you think you are. There are three ways in which we can be viewed: what we think we look like, what others think we look like, and what we actually look like. It is important to know what those differences are and bring them together so you can maximise your potential in how you look.

The first thing is to look after your body by keeping fit. Take plenty of exercise and watch what you eat across your whole diet. Go easy on the burger and chips, and try some fruit and vegetables. Having a fit body looks good in most clothes you choose.

Get your hair-style right. If it is the fashion of the time you want, make sure you choose the style that suits you, and again, ask your family or friends for their view. You may need to modify the fashion and have your own variation on it. As long as you look good and feel good, then you have achieved your goal.

Clothes are also a very important part of who you are, so choose carefully. There are so many styles and designs – you may have some trial and error before you get it right. Ask friends and family and also look at what other people wear. See how items of clothing go together to match up with the style that you want for yourself.

When you go out and buy clothing, make sure that you are paying the right price.

Paying brand name prices is only making the brand name owner rich. There are many good clothing manufacturers out there at reasonable prices. Choosing your clothing because of the label is a waste of money and will make you poor.

If money is not an issue, then the choice is yours. Still, think about what are you doing and what are you doing it for. Are you spending money to feel good yourself, or to make others feel good about you?

When you make your choice about how much you spend on clothing, make sure it is right for you and that you can afford it. When you are young, it is easy to be drawn into spending money you cannot afford, just to impress and be cool.

What you put on feet is very your important, not only for style, but for posture and healthy feet. If you have ill-fitting shoes, it may cost you in the future, in corns, bunions, and in some serious cases, problems with your ankles, knees, hip and back joints.

Have your shoes fitted by the staff in a good quality shop, and try, if possible, to choose leather. This is a natural material and helps let your feet breathe.

There are so many variations on style and form – you have to choose your shoe style to match the clothes you are wearing, and this can be costly. Get the colours right, and you can mix and match your clothes, so that you can use the same shoes for many styles of outfits.

Trainers have become an iconic fashion statement and can cost you more than they are worth. Search around and find shops that stock some good quality trainers at reasonable prices. There is no point in paying £100 for a designer label, for something that is only worth £50. It is down to you where you spend your money, but ask yourself whether you can afford to waste your money on labels.

Wellingtons, walking boots and other functional footwear have little worth in fashion, but if they do for you, be sure you are buying them for their function first, rather than for their design or colour. Otherwise, you will pay good money for that privilege.

You can, if money is not an issue, have your shoes tailor-made. It is expensive, but you will get an excellent pair of shoes. These shoe-makers can be found on the Internet or in your local telephone directory. Some of the best fashion and traditional shoe-makers are based in London and Rome. Some former Eastern bloc countries also have a good reputation for shoe making.

Some sporting events do have a strict dress code – for example hunting, pheasant shooting, and polo, and you will have to pay for the style of shoe or boot that is needed for each.

Throughout my fashion chapter, I have made a point of underlining the cost implications of paying for an iconic label that is expensive. The big fashion houses and manufacturers will encourage you to spend your money on their product. Their price tag will reflect their high profile from TV and magazine advertising, but there are many companies who make good quality products that are just as good. My point is that you do not have to be a victim of fashion. There is nothing wrong with being fashionable, but don't let the big business fashion producers take advantage of you.

If you look around at all the outlets, shops, and on the Internet for the items and styles that you want, you will save yourself a lot of money.

CHAPTER 13

Sport

As the human race has developed, the need for exercise has had to be made into an enjoyable activity. Our first hunter-gatherer ancestors were too busy catching food to worry about getting fat and having a heart attack. Thankfully, times have changed and we now go to the supermarket and buy our food, instead of chasing it with a spear.

The hunter-gatherer was able to prove himself as a provider in the food that he caught, because he became fast and fit enough to be able to outrun his next meal. He also had to outrun some predators, which added to the competitive need to survive.

The first long distance race was named after the run that Eukles made, to give the news of the Greek victory over the Persians, at Marathon. He ran the 26 miles, gave his message and then dropped dead. Pheidippides ran from Athens to Sparta to pass on the same message and, as legend goes, also dropped dead.

This story shows the power of the human spirit, and the need to succeed. If you add these qualities together, you end up with the basic needs for competitive sport. Our need to succeed is a basic one and it manifests itself in the jobs that we do or the type of sport we take up.

All of these historic activities form the base of athletics, but I would suggest that before you attempt a marathon, you do some training first!

Join an athletic club and see if there are any other athletic events that take your fancy, because there are many to choose from. There are athletic clubs around the country, not as numerous as football or rugby clubs, but are generally in main centres. You will need to research their location.

We all want to improve ourselves and improve our physical skills, and succeed in the things we do – the choice of the sport that we play will help achieve that.

Sometimes we use sport to build our self-esteem; to prove to others that we can do these challenging things, as well as to become fitter and possibly more attractive to the opposite sex.

A lot of young men want to be taller and bulkier. Height is genetic and you cannot change it, but you can change your physique. Athletics and bodybuilding are very popular and can give you a big increase in self-esteem.

The ability to catch food as a hunter a few thousand years ago, by chasing a rabbit or a wild boar, translates into running the 100 metres. Similarly, being good at football is like dodging a predator. This says that you, like your ancestors, have the need to be active and successful by testing your skills against others for food or for a trophy.

One of the fundamental necessities of sport is discipline and the ability to take instruction. This means having respect for the person who is training you. He more than likely is a volunteer, and is not getting paid to share his life and sporting experience with you.

As in all walks of life, discipline and self-discipline are needed. The discipline to study or to keep ourselves clean and tidy is helpful with the discipline of sport and how much desire we have to succeed and win. Your need to win will be matched by the need to train, and training takes discipline.

Your choice of activity may not always be a physical one – darts, snooker, or computer games may be your preference. We can't all be the same in the sport that we choose.

Although these activities are good for the people who play them, a balance of activity should be worked towards for your best physical and mental health. If you play a lot of computer games, you may tend to become isolated, because of the length of time you spend doing it. We know it is good fun, but it may be an idea to try and do a little active sport with your mates. This will enhance your health and maybe improve your interpersonal skills. It also is a way of meeting new people that you could get on with, who could also share your interest in computer games.

Darts and snooker are also fun - and if you are really good, you can earn a lot of money doing it. Being good at these two sports requires a high degree of concentration, and therefore requires the physical and mental sharpness you get from being physically fit.

Again, the balance needs to be drawn between practice and fitness, so that you can get the best out of yourself.

Playing football and rugby must be the most common forms of exercise, and can give you a high degree of fitness, depending on how seriously you take it. You can play these games at any age, and if you are extremely good, you can potentially become a professional.

It takes determination and a lot of hard work to succeed and be good at anything.

David Beckham is possibly the most well known footballer of today and he sets a good example to us all in his commitment to his job. This shows what can be achieved if we put our minds to it – and that applies to anything that we do. David Beckham's commitment is also shown by what he does for youngsters, by helping them learn to play the game at his football academies.

If you, as young men, can apply the same commitment to your sport, studies, work, and anything else you put your effort into, there is no limit to what you can achieve.

The dedication you put into sport is what people see of you. It shows them what you are capable of and will encourage them to help you to succeed.

This positive attitude and commitment can help in relationships as well, so you can develop trust with your friends and family and increase your ability to socialise and enhance your interpersonal skills.

If you are good enough and lucky enough to go to an academy, or get spotted by a top football team talent scout, you will still have needed the local teams to help you get on to the skills ladder, and raise your fitness levels. Most of the best players come from the top league youth teams and local clubs, but when we become older, we cannot all play for the premiership, so do put your best efforts into getting into your local side, because they all need new and young talent to get them the trophies of their league. You never know – a talent scout may be watching your next game!

I will not try and advise on football training, as I am not an expert, but I do know that the best players have that special kind of drive and love of the game that, as children, they practiced at home, often on their own, to improve their skills.

The playing that children do with a ball may not be deliberate skills improvement, but just the enjoyment of playing with a ball.

George Best, the Irish international and much revered Manchester United player of the 60s, used to play with his football in a narrow alleyway by his house, in a bid to control the ball at close quarters, to get the ball to do what he wanted it to do. This resulted in him being one of the best controllers of the ball on the football field.

David Beckham, too, has spent much of his training time on placing the ball where he wants it, in free kicks or passes to forward players in a goal scoring position. He is also classed as one of the best placers of the ball in modern football.

There are many players who can do amazing things with a ball, but the bottom line is that they all have dedication and a love of what they are doing.

Rugby football is also a very good sport to be involved in, as fitness and strength levels have to be high. It is sometimes thought that rugby is the thinking man's game, and that its followers only come from private and grammar school, and universities. There is probably some truth in the perception that rugby is for posh kids. This is probably because most comprehensive schools did not include rugby as a choice of sport in PE, but it should not stop the ordinary guy from playing this wonderful game. The need for good players is just as keen as in football, so don't be put off by this historical opinion.

Rugby is a much more physical game, and you can get seriously hurt, but is a lot of fun and in my view is worth the risk, but the risk aspect has to be your choice, so think it through.

There are fewer rugby clubs about compared to football, so hunt around – most big towns and cities have a club. Because there are fewer clubs, it may be harder for the recreational player to get into a side. Competition for a first team place could be high, if that is what you want, so your personal effort will also have to be high.

There is also the chance to earn a lot of money from a career in rugby. The level of pay is nowhere near as much as in football, but there are still many opportunities for sponsorship endorsements and product promotion, where payments are considerable.

There are some good rugby clubs around, so search them out, because if you have a talent, you and everyone else want to see it. There is a lot of competition, as in any other high profile sport, but the benefits are also substantial, and include world travel and an extensive social life.

Cricket, like the last two sports, has similar benefits, like money and world travel, but is not as popular in the UK as it is in places like India and Pakistan, where cricket is almost a religion.

There are clubs in most towns and teams always need more players to make the league system work. There are big county clubs, and they, too, need new talent to fight for their county championship. These county teams are hunting grounds for the national team scouts, so they can put forward the best team to play against the rest of the world, where the opportunities are endless.

Tennis also is a high money earner if you are a skilled player, but the chances of becoming good are harder. Some of the local clubs are very weak on youth training. There seems to be more focus on numbers of children joining the club to make it worthwhile for the coach, rather than on the quality of coaching given, so make sure you are getting value for money. If the quality of coaching is not very good, tell your parents or carer, so they can talk it through with the coach. Wimbledon is there for anyone to win if you are good enough, so coaching is very important.

Badminton, squash, boxing, and athletics are all sports you can enjoy at various centres near you, and have varying degrees of demand on your body. Badminton and squash are games that are fast and need constant alertness and fitness.

Boxing, on the other hand, needs high levels of fitness and stamina, and there is the potential of having your brains knocked about! There is protective headgear that you can wear that clubs will supply, and a lot of competitions insist on protection for the amateur.

This sport can result in serious brain damage over a period of time. A knockout can cause instant damage to your brain. However, this sport is also a good way of learning discipline and self-control, and you can also earn a lot of money. But you have to decide if you love the sport for itself or for the money. Weigh up the risks, and do what is right for you.

Cycling is possibly the most underrated sport, because the young do it without thinking of it as a sport – it's more of a way of getting around quickly and hanging out with friends. It's something you can do almost anywhere: on road, off road, across fields and through woods – there seems to be no limit.

There are also cycling clubs at local, county, and national level that you can join for competitive cycling. This, too, can lead to international competitions and product sponsorships.

When you go to buy your bike, do your research, as there are hundreds of types and designs to suit your type of cycling to choose from, with prices ranging from £100 to £1,000 and more. Bikes that are expensive need researching, so do shop around for them, looking at bike shops or Internet sites. Ask questions of someone who knows what they are talking about. Possibly an older cycling club member, with some experience, could be the person to talk to.

Don't be worried about phoning people for advice, as generally they are keen to help – you could potentially become another club member or be their next champion, in whichever sport you enquire about.

Golf is another sporting activity that the young are taking up. It is a very exacting and skilful game and not for the fainthearted. You will need a lot of practice, and this is not cheap. Golf lessons by a professional coach, club green fees, clubs and equipment do cost quite a bit of money. Some schools do play golf as a part of the normal sports curriculum, but it is rare.

If you are driven to learn to play golf, search out your local clubs and see what they can offer a young player, because some clubs do sponsor lessons for young players or give reduced rates on the practice range, and for the green fees. (This is the amount you pay to play a round or golf – either nine or 18 holes.)

Whichever sport you choose to play, there are some opportunities for coaching and management alongside your playing career, or when your playing career is over. This could be another way of continuing with a sport you love, but it can be competitive and any management position has the potential to be stressful.

It is important that whatever you do, it is what you want and that you enjoy doing it. Remember, you are in control of your life and the sport you choose is an important part of how you maintain your confidence, fitness and well being.

A last thought to leave you with is that, whatever you chose to do, in sport, work or play, the people who flourish and succeed are the people – no matter how bright they are - who put the work and effort into their success.

Help and Information Numbers

It takes courage to ask for help, but when a moment of need arrives, there is no need to worry. The people on the other end of the phone are friendly and there to listen to your fears and concerns, with the knowledge that what you say to them is in confidence, so you can be yourself and be open with what you tell them.

Here are some help line numbers for support and information.

Emergencies	Careline
If you are in personal danger, or have had an accident. Tel: 999 (or from your mobile): 112	Talk to a trained counsellor about any issue that is troubling you. Tel: 0845 122 8622
Childline	**Brook Advisory Centre**
Provides a helpline for children who are suffering abuse, bullying or any other issue that is troubling them. Tel: 0800 1111 Or write to: Childline, Freepost 1111, London N1 0BR	Confidential advice on sexual and contraceptive issues. Tel: 0800 0185 023

Anti-Bullying Campaign	Depression Alliance
Provides emotional support and advice for anyone suffering from bullying.	Gives help and support for those suffering from and affected by depression.
www.bullying.co.uk	Tel: 0845 123 23 20
Cruse Bereavement Care	**Children's Legal Centre**
Advice and support on the affects following the death of a loved one.	This independent charity gives help and advice on legal needs and support for parents and children.
Tel: 0800 808 1677	Freephone: 0800 783 2187 www.childrenslegal centre.com
Samaritans	**Frank**
Confidential and emotional support for anyone who may have suicidal feelings.	Free advice and information on drugs, available 24 hours a day. They can also provide information on local services and free literature.
Tel: 08457 90 90 90	Tel: 0800 77 66 00
If you find it difficult to talk, you can text and e-mail	
www.samaritans.org.uk	www.talktofrank.com

The Site.org	Family Planning Association
Online advice and information for young people with life worrying issues. www.thesite.org	Information on sexual health and contraception. Tel: 0845 310 1334
Drinkline	**Parentline Plus**
A national helpline offering confidential advice and support if you are concerned about your own drinking habits. Tel: 0800 917 8282	Support and advice for step family members. Tel: 0808 800 2222
Al Anon and Al Ateen	**Mind**
To assist those affected by the overuse of alcohol by a family member or friend. Tel: 020 7403 0888 www.al-anon.alateen.org	Advice and information on mental health issues. Tel: 0845 766 0163
Adfam	**Victim Support**
Help line providing advice for families and friends of drug users. Also provides information on access to services. www.adfam.org	This helpline gives information and support to the sufferers of any kind of crime. Tel: 0845 30 30 900 www.victimsupport.org.uk

Gay and Lesbian Switchboard	Netdoctor
24 hour help and support for people needing information about their sexuality concerns. Tel: 020 7837 7324 www.queery.org.uk	A factual website, written by doctors, providing medical information that could reduce your anxiety. www.netdoctor.co.uk
NHS Direct	**British Association of Anger Management**
The NHS website provides access to a wide range of medical and health information. www.nhsdirect.co.uk	Helpline Tel: 0845 1300 286 Also try: **Anger Management** Helpline Tel: 0208 554 9004
Mental Health Foundation	
Campaigns on mental health issues affecting all areas in society. Provides information on a wide range of issues that can lead to mental health problems. www.mentalhealth.org.uk	

USA	Australia
There are many help lines for your assistance via the **Crisis Center.**	**Lifeline** Confidential advice available 24 hours a day.
Kids Tel: (205) 328 5437 Teens Tel: (205) 328 5465	Tel: 13 11 14 Also –
www.crisiscenterblam.com www.csna.org	**Reachout** Website for young people www.reachout.com.au
Canada	**New Zealand**
Kids Help Line available 24 hours a day.	**Kidsline** Tel: 0800 543754
Tel: 800 668 6868 www.kidsline.org.ca	**Youth Line** Tel: 0800 376633
Telephone Counselling Service: Tel: 1-800-551-800 (24 hours)	
www.kidshelpphone.ca	

Republic of Ireland	Argentina
ONE2ONE Drugs and sexual health helpline for young people. Tel: (021) 427 5615 **Irish Society for Prevention of Cruelty to Children** 29 Lower Baggot Street, Dublin 2 Tel: (01) 676 7960 **Samaritans** Tel: (01) 850 60 90 90 www.samaritans.org.uk **Childline** Freephone: (01) 800 666 666 www.ispcc.ir	**Centro de la Valorizacion de la Vida Smaritanos** Cordigo del Plata Telefono de la Esperanza: 54 (0) 223 493 0430 www.telefonodelaesperanza.org **SOS un Amogo Anonimo** T: 54 (0) 114 783 8888 www.sosunamigoanonimo.org.ar
South Africa	**Befrienders Worldwide**
www.southafrica.info/services Covers all the countries help line numbers.	**www.befrienders.org** Their web site lists all participating countries, and gives their phone numbers.

Books to read for more life information

The Seven Principles of Respect by **Ken Barnes**
Ken Barnes is well known in the London black community and for his work with the young and their issues.

Unzipped by **Matt Whyman**
Matt Whyman is well known for his work on youth health issues, and has written many books on sex and health subjects.

Instant Confidence by **Paul McKenna**
Paul McKenna is a well-known hypnotist and life improvement psychologist and his book is well worth a read.

I'm OK, You're OK by **Thomas Harris**
Thomas Harris is a practising psychiatrist in America and has helped many people with his books on behaviour changing to help the individual take charge of their lives. This book is based on transactional analysis, which is the understanding of your thought and action processes and how you can change your behaviour by specific actions.

This may not be an easy read, but is well worth it, to help you understand yourself and how you tick.

Bush Craft by Ray Mears
If you are into the outdoor life, this book is for you. It will give you some useful life skills, and improve confidence and self-esteem.

Glossary Guide

Living with Parents p1-8
How life with parents can help and guide you, to maximise their knowledge to give you a broader experience before you set out on your own. Family relationships; banks; credit cards; criminal records

Living with friends p9-13
Hints on how to co-exist with your friends; household bills; problems that can arise; rent default; flat location

Living on your own and buying a home p14-20
Your own space; buying a home; borrowing money; surveyors and conveyance; budgeting; insurance; letting spare room

Caring for yourself p21-27
Food; cooking; cleaning; care of internal self; exercise

Self Esteem p28-35
Self-image; emotional changes; feeling good about yourself; doing the best for yourself; shyness; peer approval; education; style; surgery; rejection

Confidence p 36-41
Personality; shyness; social awareness; overcome inhibitions; independence; keeping fit; success; charm; anger

Sex and Sexuality p42-55
Boy to man; trying to understand women; talk to and about what girls want; geography of sex; preparing yourself for sex; homosexuality

A Cry for Help p56-61
How to handle anxiety; the need to talk; seeking help; suicide; bullying; anger

Work p62-65
Jobs and what pays well; type of job for you; education; enjoy what you do; how much you want to be paid; self-employment

Entertainment p66-71
High lighting venues for fun; types of entertainment; getting home safely; sport for fun - watch or play; places to eat; going to concerts

Holidays p72-85
Types of holidays; adventure and interactive; active family holidays; aid working; safety on holiday

Fashion p86-89
Clothes; shoes; hair; victim or not

Playing sport p90-98
Impression it gives of you; what it says about you; discipline; exercise for fun; types of sports; what sport costs